Multiple Regression:
A Primer

p. 22
45
93
115
133

TITLES OF RELATED INTEREST
FROM PINE FORGE PRESS

The Social Worlds of Higher Education: Handbook for Teaching
edited by Bernice Pescosolido and Ronald Aminzade

Adventures in Social Research: Data Analysis Using SPSS®
for Windows95/98™ Versions 7.5, 8.0, or Higher
by Earl Babbie and Fred Halley

Adventures in Criminal Justice Research, Revised Edition:
Data Analysis Using SPSS® for Windows95/98™ Versions 7.5, 8.0, or
Higher *by George Dowdall, Kim Logio, Earl Babbie, and Fred Halley*

Exploring Social Issues Using SPSS® for Windows95/98™
Versions 7.5, 8.0, or Higher *by Joseph Healey, John Boli, Earl Babbie,
and Fred Halley*

The Pine Forge Press Series in Research Methods and Statistics
edited by Kathleen S. Crittenden

A Guide to Field Research *by Carol A. Bailey*

Designing Surveys: A Guide to Decisions and Procedures
by Ronald Czaja and Johnny Blair

Social Statistics for a Diverse Society, Updated Printing
by Chava Frankfort-Nachmias

Experimental Design and the Analysis of Variance *by Robert Leik*

How Sampling Works *by Richard Maisel and Caroline Hodges Persell*

Program Evaluation *by George McCall*

**Investigating the Social World: The Process and Practice of Research,
2nd Edition** *by Russell K. Schutt*

Multiple Regression: A Primer

Paul D. Allison

Pine Forge Press
Thousand Oaks, California • London • New Delhi

For information, address:

Pine Forge Press
A Sage Publications Company
2455 Teller Road
Thousand Oaks, California 91320
(805) 499-4224
E-mail: sales@pfp.sagepub.com

SAGE Publications Ltd.   SAGE Publications India Pvt. Ltd.
6 Bonhill Street   M-32 Market
London EC2A 4PU   Greater Kailash I
United Kingdom   New Delhi 110 048 India

Production Coordinator: Windy Just
Production Editor: Wendy Westgate
Production Assistant: Stephanie Allen
Typesetter/Designer: Danielle Dillahunt
Cover Designer: Ravi Balasuriya

Printed in the United States of America

03 04 10 7 6 5

Library of Congress Cataloging-in-Publication Data

Allison, Paul David.
    Multiple regression: A primer / Paul D. Allison.
    p. cm. — (The Pine Forge Press series in research methods and statistics)
    Includes bibliographical references and index.
    ISBN 0-7619-8533-6 (pbk.: acid-free paper)
    1. Regression analysis. I. Title. II. Series.
    QA278.2 .A435 1998
    519.5'36—ddc21   98-40066

About the Author

Paul D. Allison, Ph.D., is Professor of Sociology at the University of Pennsylvania. He received his Ph.D. in sociology from the University of Wisconsin in 1976 and did postdoctoral study in statistics at the University of Chicago and the University of Pennsylvania. He has published three books and more than 25 articles on statistical methods in the social sciences. These have dealt with a wide variety of methods including linear regression, log-linear analysis, logit analysis, probit analysis, measurement error, inequality measures, missing data, Markov processes, and event history analysis. At present, his research is focused on the analysis of longitudinal data, especially with determining the causes and consequences of events. Each summer, he teaches 5-day workshops on event history analysis and categorical data analysis that draw nearly 100 researchers from around the United States. At Penn, he teaches graduate courses on event history analysis, categorical data analysis, and structural equation models with latent variables. His substantive interests include scientists' careers and theories of altruistic behavior.

About the Publisher

Pine Forge Press is an educational publisher, dedicated to publishing innovative books and software throughout the social sciences. On this and any other of our publications, we welcome your comments and suggestions.

Please call or write us at:

Pine Forge Press
A Sage Publications Company
2455 Teller Road
Thousand Oaks, CA 91320
(805) 499-4224
E-mail: sales@pfp.sagepub.com

Visit our World Wide Web site, your direct link to a multitude of online resources:

http://www.pineforge.com

To Linda: I missed you at the start but found you in time for the finish.

Contents

Series Foreword

The Pine Forge Press Series in Research Methods and Statistics, consisting of core books in methods and statistics and a series of satellite volumes on specialized topics, allows instructors the flexibility to create a customized curriculum. Authors of the volumes in the series are seasoned researchers and teachers as well as acknowledged experts in their fields. In addition to the core texts in research methods and statistics, the series offers more compact volumes focusing on sampling field research methods, survey research, and experimental design and analysis of variance.

We are proud to offer Paul D. Allison's *Multiple Regression: A Primer* as the latest entry in this latter series. Drawing on his extensive experience developing statistical methodology for the social sciences and applying regression and other statistical techniques in his own empirical research, Allison combines deep understanding with a practical sense of what is most important for the novice to know.

Written in engaging and simple language, this book is organized differently than traditional texts of regression. The first three chapters offer a nontechnical summary of the big picture and the fundamental principles necessary to be an informed practitioner and consumer of regression analyses. These principles, beyond the coverage of many introductory treatments, are amply illustrated with examples from the social science research literature. The nuts and bolts of running multiple regression analyses on the computer are covered in Chapter 4. Not until Chapters 5 and 6 does he address the topics usually covered first: bivariate regression, the formal mathematics of regression, and the underlying assumptions. The final three chapters address selected advanced topics and the relation of multiple regression to other statistical techniques.

The book is comprehensive enough to stand alone as an introductory text on multiple regression. However, it is streamlined enough for use with the Frankfort-Nachmias basic text, *Social Statistics for a Diverse Society*, for an introductory statistics course, or with Leik's volume on *Experimental Design and Analysis of Variance* for a slightly more advanced course of statistical techniques related to the general linear model.

—*Kathleen S. Crittenden*
Series Editor

Preface

What Sort of Book Is This?

As the title makes clear, this is a book about multiple regression. There are lots of books about multiple regression, however, and it's fair to ask if there is a need for another one. Not wanting to duplicate what's already been done, I have designed this book to be different from most books on the subject. Whether it fills a need remains to be seen.

One way in which this book differs from most others is that it is presented in the form of questions and answers. My hope is that this will make it easier for you to find answers to those questions that are uppermost in your mind, or that arise as you proceed through the book. Without further ado, let's proceed to some questions.

Who Is This Book For?

I've written this book primarily for undergraduate students in the social sciences who are taking their first research methods or statistics course. It is not intended to be the principal textbook for a course, but rather a supplement to other books on research methods or statistics. With that in mind, I have kept the book short, at least much shorter than most textbooks on regression. I've also used as little mathematics as possible, although the nature of the subject requires an occasional equation. Most important, my presumption in writing this book is that the vast majority of readers will be primarily *consumers*, not *producers*, of multiple regression results. You may have to run some multiple regressions for a homework assignment, but I'm not expecting that you'll become a statistical researcher. As a result, the book is organized rather differently from most multiple regression books, in ways that I'll discuss in a moment.

Besides students, I'm hopeful that this book will prove useful to anyone who needs to learn about multiple regression quickly, especially if the goal is to be able to read and comprehend published research results. That might include lawyers who want to use multiple regression to support legal arguments, government policymakers who need to understand the implications of the latest research for their own decisions, or managers who must evaluate the reports of market researchers.

How Is This Book Organized?

The book is structured so that the most essential questions are answered in the early chapters, with the less important questions relegated to the later chapters. With this organization, you can stop reading the book at end of any chapter and still feel like you've already gotten the meat of the subject. Chapter 1 is a general overview of what multiple regression is and what it's good for (and not good for). Chapter 2 tells you how to read and interpret multiple regression tables. Chapter 3 explains how to critique multiple regression results by asking a number of crucial questions about any regression model. These three chapters are the heart of the book. The remaining chapters discuss some of the practical aspects involved in doing multiple regression as well as a bit of the theory that underlies this method.

What Do I Need to Know to Be Able to Understand This Book?

This book is designed for readers who have a very basic knowledge of statistics. If you've previously taken a course in introductory statistics, you should have little or no difficulty. If you're currently taking a course in statistics or research methods, you may have already encountered all the concepts I will use in this book. I will assume, for example, that you're familiar with the mean, the standard deviation, and the correlation coefficient. I will also frequently refer to standard errors, confidence intervals, and hypothesis tests, so it's desirable to have a basic understanding of what these things are and how they're used. For a quick introduction to some of these concepts, see Lewis-Beck (1995). For a more detailed treatment, try Frankfort-Nachmias (1997).

How Should I Read This Book?

Chapter 1 presents the essential overview. For some of you, this chapter may be all you need (or want). Chapters 2 and 3 are recommended if you expect to read reports of multiple regression results. After reading these chapters, you may want to skip around among the remaining chapters. If you plan to run any multiple regressions yourself, you should definitely read Chapter 4 and possibly Chapters 7 and 8. If your aim is to understand the method in greater depth, I recommend Chapters 5, 6, and 9.

Where Can I Learn More?

Because the great bulk of material in this book is well known and widely available in textbooks, I have avoided giving detailed references. Nevertheless, you will find references for any unusual, non-standard, or controversial claims. There are also references to accessible textbooks covering more advanced topics, especially in Chapter 9. Because this book is deliberately short, you may find it helpful to consult more detailed textbooks on regression analysis. In my own college courses on regression analysis, I have at various times used the books by McClendon (1994), Mendenhall and Sincich (1996), Gujarati (1995), and Chatterjee and Price (1991). All four of these books are comprehensive treatments of regression analysis, written for students with modest mathematical backgrounds. In particular, they do not require a knowledge of matrix algebra. Another excellent text that does use matrix algebra in later chapters is Fox (1997).

Where Can I Get the Data?

Throughout the book, I make use of a small dataset containing information on income, schooling, age, and marital status for 35 persons. This dataset can be downloaded at the Pine Forge Website at www.pineforge.com. From the home page, click on Research Methods/Statistics for the Social Sciences, then click on the title for this book, *Multiple Regression: A Primer*. At that point, there will be instructions for downloading the data.

Acknowledgments

Nicholas Christakis (University of Chicago) provided many useful suggestions on an early draft of the book. Later drafts benefited greatly from the comments of Kathleen Crittenden, Joan Weber, and reviewers Mark Rodriguez (University of Illinois at Chicago), Robert Suchner (Northern Illinois University), Thomas J. Linneman (University of Washington), and Alan Neustadtl (University of Maryland at College Park). Steve Rutter and Sherith Pankratz at Pine Forge Press displayed remarkable patience at my numerous delays and helped raise my spirits when I became discouraged. Finally, I want to thank Arthur Goldberger, my econometrics professor at the University of Wisconsin, who taught me 90% of what I know about regression and served as a continuing model of clarity and insight.

1 What Is Multiple Regression?

In this chapter, we examine some of the basic characteristics of multiple regression. The aim is to give you enough information to begin to read and interpret results from multiple regression analysis. In later chapters, we'll revisit many of these questions and answers in greater detail.

1.1. What Is Multiple Regression?

Multiple regression is a statistical method for studying the relationship between a single *dependent* variable and one or more *independent* variables. It is unquestionably the most widely used statistical technique in the social sciences. It is also widely used in the biological and physical sciences.

1.2. What Is Multiple Regression Good For?

There are two major uses of multiple regression: prediction and causal analysis. In a prediction study, the goal is to develop a formula for making predictions about the dependent variable, based on the observed values of the independent variables. For example, an economist may want to predict next year's gross national product (GNP) based on such variables as last year's GNP, current interest rates, current levels of unemployment, and other variables. A criminologist may want to predict the likelihood that a released convict will be arrested, based on his age, the number of previous arrests, and the crime for which he was imprisoned.

In a causal analysis, the independent variables are regarded as causes of the dependent variable. The aim of the study is to determine whether a particular independent variable *really* affects the dependent variable, and to estimate the magnitude of that effect, if any. For example, a criminologist may have data showing that prisoners who participate in educational programs are less likely to be re-arrested after they are released. She may perform a multiple regression to see if this apparent relationship is real or if it could be explained away by the fact that the prisoners who enroll in educational programs tend to be those with less serious criminal histories.

These two uses of multiple regression are not mutually exclusive. The criminologist whose main interest is in the effect of educational programs may also use the regression model to make predictions about future arrests.

1.3. Are There Other Names for Multiple Regression?

A more complete name is *ordinary least squares multiple linear regression*. *Least squares* is the method used to estimate the regression equation. *Ordinary* serves to distinguish the simplest method of least squares from more complicated methods such as weighted least squares, generalized least squares, and two-stage least squares. *Multiple* means that there are two or more independent variables. *Linear* describes the kind of equation that is estimated by the multiple regression method. You'll often see various combinations of these words, as in "linear regression" or "least squares regression" or "OLS regression." (OLS stands for ordinary least squares.)

The term *regression* is harder to explain. One of the early uses of regression was by the English scientist Sir Francis Galton (1822-1911), who was investigating the relationship between heights of fathers and sons. Galton used a linear equation to describe that relationship. He noticed, however, that very tall fathers tended to have sons who were shorter than they were, whereas very short fathers tended to have sons who were taller than they were. He called this phenomenon "regression to the mean," and somehow that name stuck to the entire method.

You'll also see other names for the variables used in a multiple regression analysis. The dependent variable is sometimes called the *response* variable or the *outcome* variable. The independent variables may be referred to as *predictor* variables, *explanatory* variables, *regressor* variables, or *covariates*.

1.4. Why Is Multiple Regression So Popular?

Multiple regression does two things that are very desirable. For prediction studies, multiple regression makes it possible to *combine* many variables to produce optimal predictions of the dependent variable. For causal analysis, it *separates* the effects of independent variables on the dependent variable so that you can examine the unique contribution of each variable. In later sections, we'll look closely at how these two goals are accomplished.

In the last 30 years, statisticians have introduced a number of more sophisticated methods that achieve similar goals. These methods go by such names as logistic regression, Poisson regression, structural equation models, and survival analysis. Despite the arrival of these alternatives, multiple regression has retained its popularity, in part because it is easier to use and easier to understand.

1.5. Why Is Regression "Linear"?

To say that regression is linear means that it is based on a linear equation. In turn, a linear equation gets its name from the fact that if you graph the equation, you get a straight line. This is easy to see if there is a dependent variable and a single independent variable. Suppose that the dependent variable is a person's annual income, in dollars, and the independent variable is how many years of schooling that person has completed. Here's an example of a linear equation that predicts income, based on schooling:

$$INCOME = 8,000 + (1,000 \times SCHOOLING).$$

If you draw a graph of this equation, you get the straight line shown in Figure 1.1.

This simple equation makes it possible to predict a person's income if we know how many years of schooling the person has completed. For example, if a person has 10 years of schooling, we get a predicted income of $18,000:

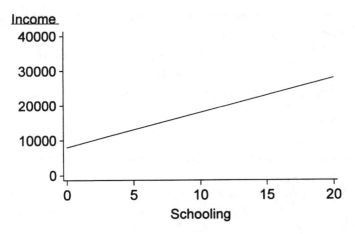

Figure 1.1. Graph of Regression Equation for Income on Schooling

$$18{,}000 = 8{,}000 + (1{,}000 \times 10).$$

Note that, according to the equation, a person with 0 years of schooling is predicted to earn $8,000. Also, each additional year of schooling increases the predicted income by $1,000.

Is it possible to get reasonable predictions from such a simple equation? Maybe and maybe not. A complete answer to this question involves many complex issues, some of which we will consider later. One issue is whether we could get better predictions with different numbers besides 8,000 and 1,000. Perhaps 9,452 and 1,789 would do better. The method of least squares is designed to find numbers that, in some sense, give us optimal predictions of the dependent variable.

We can write the two-variable linear equation in more general terms as

$$y = a + bx.$$

In this equation, y is the dependent variable and x is the independent variable. In our example, y is income and x is years of schooling. The letters a and b represent constant numbers. We call a the *intercept* and b the *slope*. These names refer to features of the graph in Figure 1.1. The intercept is the point on the vertical axis which "intercepts" the line. In other words, it is the value of y when x is 0. In this example, the intercept is 8,000. The slope tells us how big a change in y we get from a 1-unit increase in x. In this example, y goes up by $1,000 for each 1-year increase in schooling. Clearly, a larger slope corresponds to a steeper line. If the slope is 0, on the other hand, the line is perfectly flat. If the slope is negative, then an increase in x results in a *decrease* in y.

1.6. What Does a Linear Equation Look Like With More Than Two Variables?

In most applications of regression analysis, the linear equation has more than one independent variable. For prediction purposes, you can usually get better predictions if you base them on more than one piece of information. For causal analysis, you want to be able to look at the effect of one variable while *controlling* for other variables. This is accomplished by putting the other variables in the regression equation.

Suppose, for example, that we want to include age as a predictor of income. This makes sense because most people's incomes increase with age, at least until they retire. A linear equation that incorporates age might look like this:

$$INCOME = 6{,}000 + (800 \times SCHOOLING) + (400 \times AGE).$$

This equation tells us that income goes up by $400 for each additional year of age; it also goes up by $800 for each additional year of schooling. For a person who is 40 years old and has 14 years of schooling, the predicted income is

$$33{,}200 = 6{,}000 + (800 \times 14) + (400 \times 40).$$

A more general way of writing an equation with two independent variables is

$$y = a + b_1 x_1 + b_2 x_2.$$

In our example, x_1 is schooling and x_2 is age. We still call this a linear equation, although it's more difficult to draw a graph that looks like a straight line. (It would have to be a 3-dimensional graph, and the equation would be represented by a plane rather than a line.) The b's are called *slope coefficients*, but often we just call them coefficients or slopes. The essence of a linear equation is this: We multiply each variable by some number (the slope for that variable). We add those products together. Finally, we add another number (the intercept).

1.7. Why Does Multiple Regression Use Linear Equations?

We have just described the relationship between income, schooling, and age by a linear equation. Is this sensible? Maybe the real relationship is something highly nonlinear, like the following:

$$y = \left(\frac{a_1 + b_1 x_1}{a_2 + b_2 x_2} \right)^d$$

Such an equation is certainly possible. On the other hand, there is no reason to think that this nonlinear equation is any better than the linear equation. A useful general principle in science is that when you don't know the true form of a relationship, start with something simple. A linear equation is perhaps the simplest way to describe a relationship between two or more variables and still get reasonably accurate predictions. The simplicity of a linear equation also makes it much easier and faster to do the computations necessary to get good estimates of the slope coefficients and the intercept.

Even if the true relationship is *not* linear, a linear equation will often provide a good approximation. Furthermore, it's easy to modify the linear equation to represent certain kinds of nonlinearity, as we'll see in Chapter 8. Consider the relationship between age and income. Although income certainly increases with age, it probably increases more rapidly at earlier ages and more slowly at later ages, and it may eventually begin to decrease. We can represent this kind of relationship by including both age and the *square* of age in the equation:

$$\text{INCOME} = a + b_1 \text{AGE} + b_2 \text{AGE}^2.$$

Figure 1.2 shows a graph of this equation for certain values of the slopes and the intercept. Equations like this can easily be handled by any computer program that does ordinary multiple regression. Highly nonlinear equations—like the one shown earlier—require more specialized computer programs that are not so widely available.

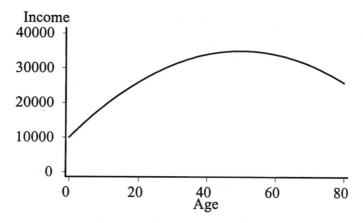

Figure 1.2. Income as a Nonlinear Function of Age

1.8. What Kinds of Data Are Needed for Multiple Regression?

To do a regression analysis, you first need a set of cases (also called units of analysis or observations). In the social sciences, the cases are most often persons, but they could also be organizations, countries, or other groups. In economics, the cases are sometimes units of time, like years or quarters. For each case, you need measurements on all the variables in the regression equation.

Table 1.1 is an example of a data set that could be used to do a multiple regression predicting income from age and years of schooling. The data come from the General Social Survey, an annual survey based on a national probability sample of U.S. adults (Davis and Smith, 1997). Table 1.1 lists a small subset of these data, specifically, all white males living in New England. The data are arranged so that each row corresponds to a case (person) and each column corresponds to a variable. For example, the first row describes a person whose income was $48,000 who had 12 years of schooling and was 54 years old. Neither the cases nor the variables have to be in any particular order. Virtually any regression program could read the data in Table 1.1 exactly as they appear.

The 35 cases in Table 1.1 are sufficient to do the multiple regression but, as in any statistical analysis, the more cases the better. For the computation to work at all, you must have at least as many cases as variables (including the dependent variable). To do a decent job,

TABLE 1.1 Data on Income, Schooling, and Age, 1983 General Social Survey

Income	Schooling	Age
48,000	12	54
26,000	12	28
26,000	7	56
48,000	14	47
13,000	14	23
34,000	12	60
18,000	11	36
24,000	16	34
81,000	16	61
21,000	12	38
9,000	6	53
18,000	12	34
34,000	13	58
21,000	14	38
81,000	12	46
48,000	20	54
6,000	7	76
21,000	14	35
21,000	12	34
9,000	14	23
34,000	14	44
7,000	9	31
24,000	8	56
34,000	16	37
34,000	17	40
4,000	12	20
5,000	9	65
13,000	14	53
7,000	20	33
13,000	12	31
34,000	7	30
10,000	16	36
48,000	18	54
6,000	12	19
2,000	10	25

you need far more than that. Most regression analysts would be reluctant to do a regression with less than five cases per variable, although there are exceptional situations when fewer cases might be enough.

The most desirable data come from a probability sample from some well-defined population, as is the case with the data in Table 1.1. In practice, people often use whatever cases happen to be available. A medical researcher, for example, may use all the patients admitted to a particular hospital in a 1-year period. An educational researcher may use all the students enrolled in a particular school. Although it is acceptable to use such "convenience samples," you must be very cautious in generalizing the results to other populations. What you find in one school or hospital may not apply to any other. Convenience samples are also more likely to violate the assumptions that justify multiple regression (see Chapter 6).

1.9. What Kinds of Variables Can Be Used in Multiple Regression?

For the data in Table 1.1, all the variables were quantitative variables. Age, income, and years of schooling are all measured on some well-defined scale. For each of these scales, it's reasonable to claim that an increase of a specified amount means the same thing no matter where you start. Thus, an increase from $20,000 to $30,000 is, in some sense, equivalent to an increase from $30,000 to $40,000. An increase from 25 to 30 years of age is comparable to an increase from 30 to 35 years of age. Variables like this, called *interval scales*, are entirely appropriate for regression analysis.

Many variables in the social sciences don't have this property. Suppose, for example, that a questionnaire includes the statement "This country needs stronger gun control laws" and then asks people whether they strongly agree, agree, disagree, or strongly disagree. The researcher assigns the following scores:

1 = strongly disagree
2 = disagree
3 = agree
4 = strongly agree.

I think most people would accept the claim that higher scores represent stronger agreement with the statement, but it's not at all clear that the distance between 1 and 2 is the same as the distance between 2 and 3, or between 3 and 4. Variables like this are called *ordinal scales*. The numbers tell you the order on some dimension of interest, but they don't tell you the magnitude of the difference between one value and another.

Strictly speaking, ordinal variables are inappropriate for multiple regression because the linear equation, to be meaningful, requires information on the magnitude of changes. In practice, however, ordinal variables are used quite often in regression analysis because there aren't good alternatives. If you use such variables, you are implicitly assuming that an increase (or a decrease) of one unit on the scale means the same no matter where you start. This might be a reasonable approximation in many cases.

Then there are variables that don't have any order at all. What do you do with a variable like gender (male or female) or marital status (never married, married, divorced, widowed)? Variables like this are called *nominal scales*. If the variable has only two categories, like gender, the solution is easy. Just assign a score of 1 to one of the categories and a score of 0 to the other category. It doesn't matter which one you choose, as long as you remember which is which. Such 1-0 variables are called *dummy variables* or *indicator variables*. Later on we'll discuss how to interpret the slope coefficients for dummy variables. We'll also see how the method of dummy variables can be extended to nominal variables with more than two categories. Dummy variables are perfectly OK as *independent* variables in a multiple regression. Although it's not fatal to use a dummy variable as a *dependent* variable in a regression analysis, there are much better methods available. The most popular alternative—known as logit analysis or logistic regression—will be briefly discussed in Chapter 9.

1.10. What Is Ordinary Least Squares?

Ordinary least squares is the method most often used to get values for the regression coefficients (the slopes and the intercept). The basic idea of least squares is pretty simple, although the computations can get quite complicated if there are many independent variables.

If we knew the values of the regression coefficients, we could use the linear equation to produce a predicted value of the dependent variable for each case in the sample. We usually don't know the true values of the coefficients, but we can try out different guesses and see which ones produce the "best" predicted values. Suppose, for example, that we make some guesses for the data in Table 1.1. Let's guess a value of zero for the intercept, $1,000 for the slope for schooling, and $500 for the slope for age. For the first case in the sample, aged 54 with 12 years of schooling, we get a predicted value of

$$0 + (1,000 \times 12) + (500 \times 54) = 39,000.$$

The observed income for this person is $48,000, so our prediction is $9,000 too low. Still, it's not bad for just guessing the coefficients. Now let's try the second person, who had 12 years of education and was 28 years old:

$$0 + (1,000 \times 12) + (500 \times 28) = 26,000.$$

Our predicted value is now identical to the observed value of $26,000. For the third person, aged 56 with 7 years of schooling, we have

$$0 + (1,000 \times 7) + (500 \times 56) = 35,000.$$

This person's observed income is $26,000, so our prediction is $9,000 too high.

We could continue generating predictions for each case in the sample. For each case we could then calculate a *prediction error*:

Error = Observed Value – Predicted Value.

Some of these errors will be positive (observed higher than predicted), and some will be negative (observed less than predicted). Some will be large and others will be small. Clearly, we would like to find coefficients that make these errors as small as possible.

For data in the social sciences, it's virtually impossible to find coefficients that make all the errors equal to zero. In our example, that would mean that we could perfectly predict every person's income just by knowing his or her age and years of schooling. Not likely. We'll have to settle for making the errors as small as we can. The problem is that if we tried out different sets of coefficients, we would find that errors for some people get larger while errors for other people get smaller. How do we balance one error against another?

There's no universally accepted answer to this question, but the most widely used method is the least squares criterion. This criterion says to

choose coefficients that make the sum of the squared prediction errors as small as possible.

For the income example, the first error was $9,000, so its square is 81,000,000. The second error was $0 so its square is 0. The third error was –$9,000 and its square is 81,000,000. Notice that squaring this third error turns a negative quantity into a positive quantity. That means that the least squares criterion doesn't care about the direction of the error, just the magnitude. On the other hand, the least squares criterion hates big errors. It would much rather have a lot of small errors than one big error.

If we continue in this way for all 35 cases, we find that the total sum of squared errors for our initial guess of the coefficients is 12,296,499,985. This may seem like a very large number, but there's no way to evaluate it without comparing it to something else. The important question is this: Can we find another set of coefficients that gives us a smaller sum of squared errors?

One way to answer this question is by trial and error. We could make a lot of different guesses for the coefficients and compute the sum of squared errors for each set of guesses. Then we could pick the one with the smallest sum. Unfortunately, the number of possible guesses is infinite, so this would not be a very efficient way to get the optimal set of coefficients. Fortunately, the best set of coefficients can be obtained directly by some straightforward but tedious calculations, best left to a computer. For the data in Table 1.1, the linear equation that minimizes the sum of squared errors is

INCOME = –25,965 + (2,057 × SCHOOLING) + (600 × AGE).

For this set of coefficients, the sum of squared errors is 9,364,695,694, which is 24% lower than the sum of squared errors for our original guesses.

This equation says that each additional year of schooling increases the predicted annual income by $2,057 and each additional year of age increases the predicted income by $600. The intercept (–$25,965) could be interpreted as the predicted income for a person who is 0 years old with 0 years of schooling. Of course, no one in this sample has anywhere near these values for age and schooling. In general, the intercept in a regression equation doesn't have a very useful interpretation, especially when values of 0 on the independent variables are far from the values that are actually observed. Still, the intercept is necessary to make the predictions come out right.

1.11. How Can We Judge How Good the Predictions Are?

Least squares regression always produces the "best" set of linear predictions for a given set of data. But sometimes the best isn't very good. It would be nice to have some way of gauging just how good the predictions are. The most common statistic for doing this is something called the *coefficient of determination*. Most people know this statistic by its symbol, R^2, pronounced *r-squared*.

The basic idea behind R^2 is to compare two quantities:

- The sum of squared errors produced by the least squares equation that you're evaluating and
- The sum of squared errors for a least squares equation with *no* independent variables (just the intercept).

When an equation has no independent variables, the least squares estimate for the intercept is just the mean (average) of the dependent variable. That implies that our predicted value for every case is the mean.

For our income example, we subtract the mean income ($25,200) from each observed income, square the result, and sum over all 35 persons. This produces a sum of squared errors of 12,947,600,000. Recall that the sum of squared errors from our equation with age and schooling was 9,364,695,694. Now divide the smaller sum by the larger sum and subtract the result from 1.0, which gives us an R^2 of .28, or 28%. To write this in symbols, let SSE be the sum of squared errors. The formula is

$$R^2 = 1 - \frac{SSE \text{ (regression)}}{SSE \text{(mean only)}}$$

We say, then, that using age and schooling to predict income yields a 28% reduction in the (sum of squared) prediction errors, compared with using only the mean. That's not bad for data in the social sciences. Alternatively, we can say that age and schooling "explain" 28% of the variation in income.

1.12. How Do We Judge How Good the Coefficient Estimates Are?

In any regression analysis, we typically want to know something about the accuracy of the numbers we get when we calculate estimates of the regression coefficients. In our income example, we got a least squares coefficient estimate of $600 for the age variable. That may be the best estimate we can get with the data, but it's unlikely to be exactly "right." As in most applications of regression analysis, there are three possible sources of error:

- Measurement error: Very few variables can be measured with perfect accuracy, especially in the social sciences.
- Sampling error: In many cases, our data are only a sample from some larger population, and the sample will never be exactly like the population.
- Uncontrolled variation: Age and schooling are surely not the only variables that affect a person's income, and these uncontrolled variables may "disturb" the relationship between age and income.

To make any headway, we have to make some assumptions about how these sources of error operate. Without going into details, the basic assumption is that the errors occur in a random, unsystematic fashion (see Chapter 6 for more about these assumptions). The result is random variation in our coefficient estimates. We evaluate the extent and importance of this random variation by calculating *confidence intervals* or *hypothesis tests*.

Confidence intervals give us a range of possible values for the coefficients. Although we may not be *certain* that the true value falls in the calculated range, we can be reasonably confident. Hypothesis tests are used to answer the question of whether or not the true coefficient is zero. Again, we never get a definitive answer, but can calculate the probability of being wrong. If you've already had a statistics course, you'll recall that the first step in getting confidence intervals and hypothesis tests is usually the calculation of the standard error (a kind of standard deviation). If you haven't had a statistics course, what follows may seem a little obscure. Still, it's essential for interpreting results from a multiple regression analysis.

Every computer program that does multiple regression will automatically calculate and report a standard error for each regression coefficient. For our income example, the coefficient for age is $600, and its standard error is $210. For the schooling coefficient ($2,057), the standard error is $849. To get a 95% confidence interval, we follow the same procedure used to construct confidence intervals around a mean: We add two standard errors to the coefficient, and then we subtract two standard errors from the coefficient. (For these data, a more precise multiplier is 2.037, but 2 is close enough unless the sample is quite small.) For age, we have $600 + (2 \times 210) = 1{,}020$ and $600 - (2 \times 210) = 180$. We then say that we are 95% confident that the true coefficient lies somewhere between $180 and $1,020. Similar calculations for the schooling coefficient produce a 95% confidence interval of $359 to $3,755.

In published research using regression analysis, you're more likely to see hypothesis tests than confidence intervals. Usually, the kind of question people most want answered is "Does this particular variable really affect the dependent variable?" If a variable has no effect, then its true coefficient is zero. When you calculate a multiple regression, you virtually never get a coefficient that's exactly zero, though you may find some that are very small. Small coefficients could easily be produced by the three kinds of random error mentioned earlier, even when the true coefficient is zero. But how small is very small, and how big does an estimated coefficient have to be for us to conclude that the true coefficient is something other than zero? That's the job of hypothesis tests—to tell us whether nonzero coefficients could have been produced by random error.

Actually, what the tests give us is not a simple yes or no answer but a *probability* or *p value*. If the *p* value is small, it's taken as evidence that the coefficient is not zero. The test is calculated by first dividing each coefficient by its standard error, producing something called a *t* statistic. Then you consult a *t* table (or the computer does this for you) to calculate the associated *p* value. Most multiple regression programs do these calculations for you, but occasionally you may find one that only reports the coefficient and its standard error, in which case you'll have to determine the *p* value yourself by referring to a *t* table, which is displayed and explained in any introductory statistics text.

For our income example, if you divide the coefficient for age by its standard error (600/210), you get a *t* statistic of 2.86. This has an associated *p* value of .007, which has the following interpretation: If the true coefficient for age is 0, the probability of estimating a coefficient larger than 600 (or smaller than −600) would be about .007, or about one in 150. For schooling, the t statistic has a value of 2.42, with an associated p value of .02. Again, we can say that if the true coefficient for schooling is zero, the probability of estimating a coefficient this much different from zero is .02. In general, the smaller the p value, the stronger the evidence that the coefficient is *not* zero.

Are these p values small enough to conclude that the true coefficients for age and schooling are something other than zero? There's no absolute rule about this: It depends on the situation, especially on the cost of making an error of one sort or another. Because these costs are difficult to quantify, social researchers usually don't think much about this. Instead, they rely on the customary standards of .05 and .01. If the p value is less than .05, we say that the coefficient is "significantly different from zero" and conclude that there is evidence for a nonzero coefficient. If the p value is less than .01, we say that the coefficient is "highly significant" and conclude that there is strong evidence for a nonzero coefficient. Even though there's probably too much reliance on these rote standards, you won't go far wrong by using them.

1.13. How Does Multiple Regression "Control" for Variables?

It's easy to see why multiple regression might be good for making predictions: It's explicitly designed to make errors of prediction as small as possible (using the least squares criterion for overall smallness). Earlier, I claimed that another major use of multiple regression is to examine the effects of some independent variables on the dependent variable while "controlling" for other independent variables. In our income example, the coefficient for years of schooling can be interpreted as the effect of schooling on income while controlling for age or "holding age constant." Similarly, the coefficient for age can be interpreted as the effect of age on income while controlling for years of schooling.

In what sense does multiple regression control for variables, and how does it do it? This is a complex and subtle question, and I can only hope to scratch the surface in this chapter. Many practicing researchers just accept it on faith that multiple regression controls for variables. The issue is also somewhat controversial. There are some statisticians who take the conservative position that only a randomized experiment can *really* control for extraneous variables, and that multiple regression is, in most cases, only a poor approximation.

With that in mind, let's first see how an experiment controls for extraneous variables. Suppose, for example, that we want to evaluate the effectiveness of a training course to raise SAT scores (the dependent variable). We give the course to some people and withhold it from others. Then we compare how well they do on the test. For this to be a valid experiment, we have to make sure that people in the two groups are treated exactly the same, except for the training course. For example, it wouldn't be a fair comparison if people who didn't get the training took the SAT exam in a hot, noisy room while those who got the training took their exams in a comfortable room.

All the conditions that affect performance must be equalized for the two groups. Even if we were successful at doing that, there's still the problem that people in the two groups might be different. Maybe those who got the training are smarter than those who didn't. We certainly can't force people to be equally intelligent, but what we *can* do is randomly assign people to one group or the other. For each person recruited into the study, we could flip a coin to decide if they should be in the treatment group or the control group. With random assignment, the two groups will, on average, be the same on all possible characteristics: age, sex, race, intelligence, ambition, anxiety, and so on.

With observational (nonexperimental) studies, we don't have those options for ensuring that our comparison groups are comparable. Suppose, for example, that we do a survey of 10,000 college freshmen and we ask them for their SAT scores. We also ask them if they ever took an SAT training course. At this point, the damage is already done. Those who took SAT training may be very different in other respects from those who did not. A simple comparison of average SAT scores for those who did and did not take SAT training could easily give us very misleading results.

The situation is not hopeless, however, because we can still do *statistical* controls. For example, there is plenty of evidence that people with a strong high school grade point average (GPA) do better on the SAT than those with a lower high school GPA. If people with high GPAs were more likely to take SAT training, it could look like people with the training did better even though the training itself had no effect. If we know the students' high school GPAs, we can restrict our comparisons to those who have the same, or nearly the same, GPA. Suppose, for example, that our sample contained 500 students with high school GPAs that were exactly 3.00, and that 100 of these students took an SAT training course. Then, if we compare the SAT scores of these 100 students with the 400 students who did not get SAT training, we could be reasonably confident that our comparison was not contaminated by differences in high school GPA.

We could do the same sort of statistical control for any other variable. We know, for example, that males tend to do better than females on the math component of the SAT. For a valid comparison of SAT training versus no training, therefore, we should restrict our sample to males only or females only.

Although this is a very useful method, it has several rather obvious limitations. First, unless the sample is very large, it may be difficult to find a substantial number of people who are identical, or even very similar, on the control variable. It may not be too hard for a variable like gender that has only two values, but it can be very difficult for variables measured on a continuum, like GPA or income. In our SAT study, for example, if we only had 500 cases to start with, we might find only 10 people who had GPAs of exactly 3.00. Of those 10, perhaps only 2 got SAT training. That's hardly enough cases to make a reliable comparison. Instead of requiring that people have *exactly* the same GPAs, we could instead take all people who have, say, between 3.0 and 3.5, but that reduces the effectiveness of the control and could still allow for some contaminating effect of GPA differences on SAT performance.

The second problem is an extension of the first. If we only control for sex, the SAT scores could still be contaminated by differences in GPA. If we only control for GPA, the results could be due to sex differences. It's not good enough to control one variable at a time. We really need to control simultaneously for gender, GPA, socioeconomic status, and everything else that might affect SAT performance. To do this statistically, we would need to find a group of people who have the same gender, the same GPA, the same socioeconomic status, and so on. Even if we had a sample of 1 million college freshmen, it would be hard to isolate any group that was exactly alike on all these variables.

There is a third problem with this method of statistical control, but one that can also be seen as an advantage. If we restrict our sample to those with GPAs of 3.0, we might find only a trivial difference between the average SAT scores of those who got training and those who did not. If we look only at those with GPAs of 2.0, we might find a substantial difference in the SAT performance of those with and without training. Now maybe this simply reflects reality. It's quite plausible that SAT training might be more useful for poorer students than for better students. On the other hand, it could also be just random variation, in which case our interpretation of the results has been needlessly complicated. If we divide the sample into many different groups, with the people in each group being approximately the same on the control variables, we may end up with a very complicated pattern of results. Fortunately, this problem has a simple solution: Within each group of people who are nearly the same on the control variables, we compute the "effect" of SAT training (the difference between the average SAT scores of those who did and those who did not get training); then we average those effects across the groups (possibly weighting by the size of the group). Thus, if men show an average gain of 20 points from SAT training and women show an average gain of 10 points from SAT training, and if there are equal numbers of men and women, the overall estimate for the effectiveness of training would be a 15 point gain. Of course, you may not want to compute such an average if you have reason to think that the effects are really different for men and women.

What does this long-winded digression have to do with multiple regression? Well, multiple regression can be seen as just an extension of the basic logic of statistical control, but one that solves the three problems discussed above. It enables us to control for variables like GPA even though no two people in the sample have exactly the same GPA. It allows for the simultaneous control of many variables even though no two people are exactly alike on all the variables. And it only gives us a single estimate for the "effect" of each variable, which is analogous to the weighted average of effects in different subgroups. Exactly how it does all these things is beyond the scope of this chapter. See Chapter 5 for more details.

1.14. Is Multiple Regression as Good as an Experiment?

Compared to the cruder methods of statistical control (finding homogeneous subgroups and making comparisons within subgroups), multiple regression has clear advantages. Those advantages are purchased at some cost, however. To solve the three problems of the crude methods, we have to make some assumptions about the form of the relationship between the independent variables and the dependent variable. Specifically, as we saw earlier in the chapter, we have to assume that those relationships can be described, at least approximately, by a linear equation. If that assumption is incorrect, multiple regression could give us misleading results.

Multiple regression shares an additional problem with *all* methods of statistical control, a problem that is the major focus of those who claim that multiple regression will never be a good substitute for the randomized experiment. To statistically control for a variable, you have to be able to *measure* that variable so that you can explicitly build it into the data analysis, either by putting it in the regression equation or by using it to form homogeneous subgroups. Unfortunately, there's no way that we can measure all the variables that might conceivably affect the dependent variable. No matter how many variables we include in a regression equation, someone can always come along and say, "Yes, but you neglected to control for variable X and I feel certain that your results would have been different if you had done so."

That's not the case with randomization in an experimental setting. Randomization controls for *all* characteristics of the experimental subjects, regardless of whether those characteristics can be measured. Thus, with randomization there's no need to worry about whether those in the treatment group are smarter, more popular, more achievement oriented, or more alienated than those in the control group (assuming, of course, that there are enough subjects in the experiment to allow randomization to do its job effectively).

There's a more subtle aspect to this problem of statistical control: It's not enough to be able to measure all the variables that we want to control. We also have to measure them *well*. That means that if two people get the same score on some variable, they should really be the same on the underlying characteristic that we're trying to measure. If they're not the same, then we're not really holding that variable constant when we include it in a regression model or create what we think are homogeneous subgroups. That may not be a serious problem when we're dealing with variables like gender or age (based on official records), but there are lots of "fuzzy" variables in the social sciences that we can measure only crudely, at best, among them intelligence, depression, need for achievement, marital conflict, and job satisfaction. Moreover, even those variables that we can measure precisely are often only "proxies" for variables that are much more subtle and difficult to measure. Thus, gender may be a proxy for cumulative differences in socialization between men and women.

Of course, the quality of measurement is always a matter of degree. No variable is ever measured perfectly, but some variables are measured much more accurately than others. As the quality of the measurement gets worse, the effectiveness of statistical controls deteriorates.

Does this mean, as some critics claim, that multiple regression is worthless for drawing conclusions about causal relationships? I think that's much too strong a reaction to these problems. Randomized experiments have been around only for the last century, but human beings have been making causal inferences from nonexperimental data for as long as there have been human beings. Although there have been plenty of mistaken conclusions, there have also been lots of valid conclusions. Multiple regression (and other forms of statistical control) can be seen as ways of improving on the informal and intuitive kinds of causal reasoning that go on in everyday life. There are simply too many areas in which randomized experiments are infeasible or unethical for us to reject nonexperimental data as a source of causal inference.

The most important component of any causal reasoning is the process of ruling out alternative explanations. Multiple regression is certainly very helpful in this process. Maybe it can't rule out *all* alternative explanations, but science—like life itself—is a matter of incremental improvements (punctuated by occasional radical leaps forward). When critics come up with a persuasive argument as to why some particular relationship might be spurious, it then becomes the task of the researcher to measure that potentially confounding variable and include it in the regression model. There *are* limits to the number of persuasive counterarguments that critics come up with.

Chapter Highlights

1. Multiple regression is used both for predicting outcomes and for investigating the causes of outcomes.

2. The most popular kind of regression is ordinary least squares, but there are other, more complicated regression methods.

3. Ordinary multiple regression is called linear because it can be represented graphically by a straight line.

4. A linear relationship between two variables is usually described by two numbers, the slope and the intercept.

5. Researchers typically assume that relationships are linear because it's the simplest kind of relationship and there's usually no good reason to consider something more complicated.

6. To do a regression, you need more cases than variables, ideally lots more.

7. Ordinal variables are not well represented by linear regression equations.

8. Ordinary least squares chooses the regression coefficients (slopes and intercept) to minimize the sum of the squared prediction errors.

9. The R^2 is the statistic most often used to measure how well the dependent variable can be predicted from knowledge of the independent variables.

10. To evaluate the least squares estimates of the regression coefficients, we usually rely on confidence intervals and hypothesis tests.

11. Multiple regression allows us to statistically control for measured variables, but this control is never as good as a randomized experiment.

Questions to Think About

1. For a sample of 13 hospitals, a researcher measured 100 different variables describing each hospital. How many of these variables can be put in a regression equation?

2. Which is more important in describing the relationship between two variables, the slope or the intercept?

3. Suppose you want to use regression to describe the relationship between people's age and how many hours a week they watch television. Which one should be the dependent variable and which one the independent variable? Is the relationship likely to be linear?

4. For a sample of 200 U.S. cities, a linear regression is estimated with percentage of people unemployed as the dependent variable and the percentage foreign born as the independent variable. The regression slope is .20. How would you interpret this number?

5. A researcher in a college admissions department runs a regression to predict college GPA based on information available on students' applications for admission (e.g., SAT scores, high school GPA, number of advanced placement courses). The R^2 for this regression is .15. Do you think this regression model would be useful for admission decisions?

6. Based on survey data, a psychologist runs a regression in which the dependent variable is a measure of depression and independent variables include marital status, employment status, income, gender, and body mass index (weight/height^2). He finds that people with higher body mass index are significantly more depressed, controlling for the other variables. Has he proven that being overweight causes depression? Why or why not?

2 How Do I Interpret Multiple Regression Results?

If you read published articles in the social or biomedical sciences, you will inevitably encounter tables that report results from multiple regression analysis. Many of those tables are relatively simple, whereas others may be very complex. In this chapter, we examine multiple regression tables taken from five different articles that appeared in the *American Sociological Review*—arguably the leading journal in the field of sociology—and we shall see how to make sense of them. I chose these tables because they are fairly typical of what you'll find in social science journals, *not* because I thought they were examples of good research. In this chapter, we will be concerned only with what the tables mean, not whether they give correct answers to the research questions. Chapter 3 will be devoted to critiquing these and other studies.

2.1. How Does Education Promote Better Health?

Many studies have shown that more educated people tend to be in better health than less educated people. But why? Is it because educated people have better access to medical care, better work situations, or better lifestyles, or is there some other reason? Ross and Wu (1995) set out to answer this question by analyzing data from a 1990 telephone survey of 2,031 adults in the United States. Table 2.1 is one of several tables of multiple regression results that appeared in their article.

In Table 2.1, we see results from estimating two different regression equations. For both equations, the dependent variable, self-

TABLE 2.1 Self-Reported Health Regressed on Education, Controlling for Sociodemographic Characteristics (Equation 1) and Work and Economic Conditions (Equation 2)

Variable	Equation 1		Equation 2	
	b	Beta	b	Beta
Education	.076***	.220	.041***	.121
	(.007)		(.007)	
Sex (male = 1)	.114**	.062	.051	.028
	(.038)		(.038)	
Race (White = 1)	.239***	.089	.168**	.062
	(.056)		(.054)	
Age (in years)	−.013***	−.247	−.012***	−.226
	(.001)		(.001)	
Marital status	.105**	.058	.043	.024
(married = 1)	(.040)		(.037)	
Employed full-time[a]			.174***	.098
			(.044)	
Employed part-time[a]			.109	.038
			(.064)	
Unable to work[a]			−.835***	−.150
			(.114)	
Household income			.001	.040
			(.001)	
Economic hardship			−.172***	−.133
			(.028)	
Work fulfillment			.158***	.134
			(.024)	
Constant	3.413		3.729	
R^2	.152		.234	

SOURCE: Table adapted from Ross and Wu (1995). Reprinted by permission.
NOTE: N = 2,031; b = unstandardized regression coefficient with standard error in parentheses; Beta = standardized regression coefficient.
a. Compared to not employed (for reasons other than health).
*$p < .05$; **$p < .01$; ***$p < .001$ (two-tailed tests).

reported health, is "the respondent's subjective assessment of his or her general health" (coded 1 = *very poor*, 2 = *poor*, 3 = *satisfactory*, 4 = *good*, and 5 = *very good*). What distinguishes the two equations is the number of variables: Equation 1 has five independent variables, whereas Equation 2 has six additional variables. For each equation, two columns of numbers are shown, one labeled "*b*" and the other labeled "Beta." As stated in the footnote to the table, the "*b*" column contains the usual regression coefficients along with their estimated standard errors in parentheses. The "Beta" column contains *standardized coefficients*, which I'll explain a little later in this section.

We'll discuss the reason for having two different equations in a moment. For now, let's focus on the variables and results in Equation 1. Education is simply the number of years of formal schooling completed by the respondent. Equation 1 also controls for four demographic characteristics, three of which are dummy variables. Sex is coded 1 for males and 0 for females; race is coded 1 for whites and 0 for nonwhites; and marital status is coded 1 for married (or cohabiting) and 0 for everyone else. The fourth demographic variable, age, is the reported age in years at the time of the survey.

The estimated regression coefficient for education in Equation 1 is .076. We can interpret that number like this: With each additional year of education, self-reported health goes up, on average, by .076 points. Is this a large or a small number? One way to answer that question is to determine whether or not the coefficient is statistically significant. You'll notice that many of the numbers have asterisks, or stars, after them. This is a common (but not universal) way to show which coefficients are significantly different from zero. As shown in the footnotes to the table, a single asterisk indicates a coefficient whose p value is less than .05, two asterisks signal a coefficient whose p value is less than .01, and three asterisks means that the p value is less than .001. In this table, we see that the coefficient for education has three stars in both Equations 1 and 2. The interpretation is this: If education really has no effect on self-rated health, the probability of finding a coefficient as large or larger than the least squares estimate is less than one in a thousand. All the variables in Equation 1 have statistically significant coefficients. In Equation 2, all the coefficients are significant except for sex, marital status, household income, and employed part-time.

If the stars were omitted from the table, we could still determine the statistical significance of the variables by simple hand calculations. Beneath each coefficient is the standard error (in parentheses). If we divide each coefficient by its standard error, we get the t statistic discussed in Chapter 1. For example, in Equation 2, the t statistic for sex is $.051/.038 = 1.34$. Because the sample size is so large $(N = 2,031)$, the t statistic has a distribution that is essentially a standard normal distribution. Referring to a normal table (which can be found in any introductory statistics book), we find that the p value for the sex coefficient is .09. Because this is not markedly higher than the criterion value of .05, it would be unwise to completely dismiss this variable.

There's more to life than statistical significance, however. To get a better idea of what the coefficient of .076 for education means, it's essential to have a clear understanding of the units of measurement for the dependent and independent variables. Recall that self-rated health is measured on a 5-point scale and education is measured in years of schooling. We say, then, that each 1-year increase in schooling is associated with an increase of .076 in self-rated health. This implies that it would take 13 = 1/.076 additional years of schooling to achieve a 1-point increase in self-rated health (e.g., moving from "satisfactory" to "good"). To me, this does not seem like a very large effect.

Remember that the estimate of .076 "controls" for sex, race, age, and marital status. Thus, it tells us what happens when years of schooling changes but all the other variables remain the same. In the same way, each of the coefficients represents the effect of that variable controlling for all the others. The coefficient for age of −.013 in Equation 1 tells us that each additional year of age reduces self-rated health by an average of .013 points on the 5-point scale. Again, although this coefficient is highly statistically significant, the effect is not very large in absolute terms. A 10-year increase in age yields only a tenth of a point reduction in self-rated health.

The other variables in the equation are dummy variables, coded as either 1 or 0. As we saw in Chapter 1, this is a standard way of incorporating dichotomous variables in a regression equation. The coefficient for a dummy variable is like any other coefficient in that it tells us how much the dependent variable changes for a 1-unit increase in the independent variable. For a dummy variable, however, the only way to get a 1-unit increase is to go from 0 to 1. That implies that the coefficient can be interpreted as the average value of the dependent variable for all the people with a value of 1 on the dummy variable minus the average value of the dependent variable for all the people with a 0 on the dummy variable, controlling for the other variables in the model. For this reason, such coefficients are sometimes described as adjusted differences in means. For example, males have self-rated health that averages .114 points higher than females, whites have self-rated health that's about .239 points higher than nonwhites, and married people have self-rated health that's .104 points higher than that of single people.

Equation 2 adds several more variables that describe work status and economic status. Household income is measured in thousands of dollars per year. Its coefficient is small and not statistically significant. Economic hardship is an index constructed by averaging responses to three questions, each measured on a 4-point scale. Not surprisingly, those who report a high degree of economic hardship have lower self-rated health. Work fulfillment is also an average of responses to three questions that are each measured on a 5-point scale. Those who report greater fulfillment have higher self-rated health. Because these two variables have units of measurement that are rather unfamiliar, it is difficult to interpret the numerical magnitudes of their coefficients.

There are three dummy variables in Equation 2 that describe work status: employed full-time, employed part-time, and unable to work. Each of these is coded 1 or 0 depending on whether or not the person is in that particular status or not. There are actually four categories of employment status that are mutually exclusive and exhaustive: employed full-time, employed part-time, unable to work, and not employed (for reasons other than health). As explained in Chapter 8, we can't put dummy variables for all four categories in the regression equation, because this would lead to a situation of *extreme multicollinearity*. Instead, we choose one of them to leave out of the model (in this case, not employed). We call the excluded category the *reference category* because each of the coefficients is a comparison between an included category and the reference category. For example, those employed full-time average .174 points higher in self-rated health than those who are unemployed. Those who are unable to work have self-rated health that is .835 points *lower*, on average, than those who are unemployed. This is hardly surprising because the main reason that people are unable to work is because of poor health. Those employed part-time have slightly better health (.109) than those who are unemployed, but the difference is not statistically significant.

Why did the authors of this study estimate two different regression equations for the same dependent variable? They were trying to answer this question: How much of the association between education and self-rated health can be "explained" by their relationships with other variables? By comparing the coefficients for education in Equation 1 and Equation 2, we can see how the effect of education changes when we control for employment status and economic well-being. Specifically, we see that the education coefficient is cut almost in half when other variables are introduced into the equation. This tells us that the employment and income variables play an important role in mediating the impact of education on self-rated health. In the original article, the authors also reported two other equations for self-rated health that are not shown here. One equation added two variables measuring "social psychological resources," and the other added two more variables measuring "health lifestyle." When these variables were included, the coefficient for education declined even further, but the declines were not as big as when the employment and economic variables were added. In the model with all the independent variables, the coefficient for education was .031.

Now let's consider the standardized (Beta) coefficients that are reported in the second column for each of the two equations. These statistics are often reported in social science journals. As we've seen, *unstandardized* coefficients depend greatly on the units of measurement for the independent and dependent variables. That makes it hard to compare coefficients for two different variables that are measured in different ways. How can you compare, for example, a 1-unit increase on the economic hardship scale with a change from unmarried to married? Standardized coefficients solve that problem by putting everything into a common metric: standard deviation units. The standardized coefficients tell us how many standard deviations the dependent variable changes with an increase of one standard deviation in the independent variable. For example, in Equation 1 we see that an increase of one standard deviation in years of schooling produces an increase of .220 standard deviations in self-reported health. By comparing standardized coefficients across different variables, we can get some idea of which variables are more or less "important." In both equations, we see that age has the largest standardized coefficient. On the other hand, marital status has the smallest effect in both equations.

A few other things in Table 2.1 are worth noticing. The row labeled "Constant" gives estimates of the intercepts in the two equations. As usual, the intercepts don't tell us much that's interesting. In Equation 1, the intercept is 3.413. That's our estimate of the self-rated health of someone with a value of 0 on all the independent variables. In words, that person is female, nonwhite, and unmarried, with 0 years of schooling and age 0. The lesson here is that you shouldn't pay much attention to the intercept estimates.

The next row is R^2, which is our measure of how well we can predict the dependent variable knowing only the independent variables in the model. For Equation 1, the R^2 is only .15, whereas for Equation 2 it rises to .23. This means that the five variables in Equation 1 "explain" about 15% of the variation in self-rated health. When we add in the other six variables, we can explain about 23% of the variation in self-rated health. Thus, even though nearly all these variables have coefficients that are statistically significant, they account for only a small portion of the variation. Either many other factors also affect self-rated health, or else there's lots of random measurement error in self-rated health scores.

Unfortunately, many researchers put too much emphasis on R^2 as a measure of how "good" their models are. They feel terrific if they get an R^2 of .75, and they feel terrible if the R^2 is only .10. Although it is certainly true that higher is better, there's no reason to reject a model if the R^2 is small. As we see in this example, despite the small R^2 in Equation 1, we still got a clear confirmation that education affects self-rated health. On the other hand, it's quite possible that a model with a high R^2 could be a terrible model: The wrong variables could be in the model, or other assumptions could be violated (more on that in the next chapter).

2.2. Do Mental Patients Who Believe That People Discriminate Against Them Suffer Greater Demoralization?

Based on labeling theory, Link (1987) hypothesized that mental patients who believe that people generally devalue and discriminate against mental patients will experience greater levels of "demoralization." For a sample of 174 mental patients, he administered a 12-item devaluation-discrimination scale that included such statements as "Most people would willingly accept a former mental patient as a close friend." Scores on this scale ranged from 1 to 6, with 6 representing the most devaluation.

At the same time, the patients completed a 27-item scale designed to measure "demoralization." The questions dealt with such themes as low self-esteem, helplessness, hopelessness, confused thinking, and sadness. Several other variables were also measured so that they could be controlled in the regression analysis.

TABLE 2.2 Effect of the Devaluation and Discrimination Measure on
Demoralization in First- and Repeat-Contact Patients

	Unstandardized Regression Coefficient	Standardized Regression Coefficient	t Value	Significance
Control variables				
Married (1) vs. unmarried (0)	−.322	−.163	−2.380	.018
Hispanic (1) vs. other (0)	.345	.173	2.515	.013
Hospitalized (1) vs. never hospitalized (0)	.377	.227	3.163	.002
Diagnosis of depression (1) vs. schizophrenia (0)	.486	.303	4.223	.000
Test Variable				
Devaluation-discrimination	.211	.232	3.35	.001
$R^2 = .232$				

SOURCE: Table adapted from Link (1987). Reprinted by permission.
NOTE: $N = 174$.

Table 2.2 gives results for a multiple regression in which demoralization was predicted by devaluation-discrimination and other variables. The table is presented almost exactly in the form it appeared in the *American Sociological Review*. The table divides the independent variables into "Control Variables" and "Test Variable." This merely reflects the author's primary interest in the effect of the devaluation-discrimination variable. The multiple regression procedure itself makes no distinction among the independent variables.

Let's look first at the last column, labeled "Significance." This is the p value for testing the hypothesis that a coefficient is equal to 0. Because all the p values are less than .05, we learn that all the coefficients in the table are statistically significant, some of them highly significant. Reporting the exact p value is considerably more informative than just putting asterisks next to the coefficients.

It's no accident that all the variables in the model are statistically significant. In a footnote, Link explains that he originally put three other control variables in the regression equation: sex, years of education, and employment status. Because they were not statistically significant, he deleted them from the model and re-estimated the regression equation. This is a common, but not universal, practice among regression analysts. Those who do it argue that it simplifies the results and improves the estimates of the coefficients for the variables that remain in the equation. On the other side are those who claim that letting statistical significance determine which variables stay in the regression equation violates assumptions needed for calculating p values. In most cases, it doesn't make much difference one way or the other.

Link's hypothesis is supported by the positive, statistically significant coefficient for devaluation-discrimination. Those patients who believe more strongly that mental patients are discriminated against do seem to experience greater levels of demoralization. This relationship holds up even when we control for other factors that affect demoralization.

The column labeled "unstandardized regression coefficients" contains the usual regression coefficients. Devaluation-discrimination has a coefficient of .211, which tells us that each 1-unit increase on the devaluation-discrimination scale is associated with an increase of .211 units on the demoralization scale, controlling for the other variables in the model. Again, to get a sense of what this number means, we need to have some appreciation of the units of measurement for these two variables. As already noted, the devaluation-discrimination scale ranges from 1 to 6. Its mean is around 4, and its standard deviation is close to 1. The article doesn't indicate the range of possible values for the demoralization scale, but it does tell us that the mean is approximately 3 and the standard deviation is about .75. That tells us that about 95% of the sample is between 1.5 and 4.5 on this scale. For both these variables, then, a 1-unit change is pretty substantial. With this in mind, we interpret the coefficient of .211 as telling us that a moderately large change in devaluation-discrimination produces a modest, but not small, change in demoralization.

The four control variables in this regression model are all dummy variables, having values of either 0 or 1. The coefficient of −.322 for the dummy variable for marital status indicates that, on average, married patients score .322 points lower on the demoralization scale compared with those who are not married. The coefficients for other dummy variables have a similar interpretation. Hispanics average

.345 points higher on the demoralization scale than non-Hispanics. Those patients who had been hospitalized averaged .377 points higher than those never hospitalized. Finally, patients with a diagnosis of depression averaged .486 points higher on the demoralization scale than those diagnosed as schizophrenic. For any one of these variables, if we changed the 1s to 0s and the 0s to 1s, the sign of the coefficient would change, but the magnitude would be exactly the same.

The standardized coefficient of .232 for devaluation-discrimination tells us that an increase of one standard deviation in devaluation-discrimination produces an increase of .232 standard deviations on the demoralization scale. The standardized coefficient for diagnosis tells us that an increase of one standard deviation in the diagnosis variable produces an increase of .303 standard deviations in demoralization. We can therefore say that, for this sample, diagnosis is slightly more "important" than beliefs about discrimination in accounting for variation in demoralization. The smallest standardized coefficient belongs to marital status, so we can say that this variable is least important among the five variables in the model.

The column labeled t value is the test statistic for the null hypothesis that each coefficient is zero. As noted in Chapter 1, this is calculated by dividing each coefficient by its standard error. The results are then referred to a t table to determine the p values in the last column. Although this table does not report standard errors, they can easily be calculated from the t values. If you divide each (unstandardized) coefficient by its t value, you get the standard error. For devaluation-discrimination, we have $.211/3.35 = .063$. Multiplying this by 2, and then adding and subtracting the result from the coefficient (.211), produces a 95% confidence interval for the coefficient: .085 to .336. Thus, we can be 95% confident that the true coefficient for devaluation-discrimination lies somewhere between these two numbers.

2.3. Are People in Cities More Racially Tolerant?

In 1987, Tuch published a paper in the *American Sociological Review* which attempted to determine whether people who lived in large cities were less prejudiced toward blacks than people who

TABLE 2.3 Regression of Tolerance Index on Urbanism, Region, and Compositional Variables in Selected Years, 1972-1985 (Unstandardized Coefficients)

Independent Variables	Year			
	1972 (N = 982)	1977 (N = 1,118)	1982 (N = 1,063)	1985 (N = 553)
Children (1 = under 18)	−.11	−.08	.00	−.01
Income	.02	.02*	.02*	.00
Sex (1 = male)	−.01	−.03	−.07	−.03
Age	−.01**	−.01**	−.01**	−.01**
Marital status (1 = married)	−.17**	−.06	−.03	.05
Education	.07**	.08**	.07**	.09**
Urbanism (1 = urban)	.20**	.11*	.16**	.36**
Region (1 = non-South)	.53**	.49**	.49**	.30**
R^2	.28	.30	.27	.26

SOURCE: Table adapted from Tuch (1987). Reprinted by permission.
*$p < .05$; **$p < .01$.

lived in smaller towns or rural areas. He used data from several years of the General Social Survey, an annual survey of adults in the United States that is based on a large probability sample. His dependent variable was a tolerance index, which was a weighted sum of responses to five different questions. One question, for example, was "Do you think there should be laws against marriages between blacks and whites?"

Tuch divided the sample into two groups: those living in cities with 50,000 people or more (urban), and those living in cities or towns with less than 50,000 people (nonurban). He found that in 1985, the urbanites had a mean tolerance index of 13.95, whereas the nonurbanites had a mean tolerance index of 12.59, for a statistically significant difference of 1.36. Although that difference supports the hypothesis, we also know that people in urban areas differ in many ways from those in nonurban areas. There are more urban areas in the North than in the South, for example, so the urban-rural difference could merely be an artifact of the historically greater racial prejudice in the South. Tuch therefore did a multiple regression to control for region and many other factors. The results are shown in Table 2.3, which contains the information from the table in his published article. The title of this table has a common form: "Regression of y on x and z." The convention is that the variable following "of" is the dependent variable, and the variables following "on" are the independent variables.

Table 2.3 displays results from four different regressions predicting the tolerance index. The same variables are in each regression, but they're measured for completely different samples of people in four different years. The reason for doing this is to see whether the results are stable over time.

The main variable of interest—urbanism—is a dummy variable that has a value of 1 for those in urban areas and a value of 0 for those in nonurban areas. There are four other dummy variables in these regression models: children (1 = respondent has children under the age of 18, 0 = no children under 18), sex (1 = male, 0 = female), marital status (1 = married, 0 = unmarried), and region (1 = non-South, 0 =South).

As in Table 2.1, one asterisk indicates a coefficient that is statistically significant at the .05 level and two asterisks indicate a coefficient that is statistically significant at the .01 level. We see that urbanism is highly significant in all four years, with a coefficient ranging from a low of .11 to a high of .36. All four coefficients are positive, which tells us that urban people express more tolerance than nonurban people. If we recoded this variable so that 0 meant urban and 1 meant nonurban, then the four coefficients for urbanism would have the same numerical value, but all would be negative.

What can we learn from the numerical values of these urbanism coefficients? Let's consider the 1985 coefficient of .36. As we saw in the previous example, the coefficient for a dummy variable can be interpreted as an adjusted difference in the mean value of the dependent variable for the two groups, controlling for the other variables in the model. On average, then, urban residents have tolerance scores that are .36 higher than nonurban residents, controlling for the other variables in the model. Earlier we saw that the unadjusted difference in the mean tolerance scores for urban and nonurban residents was 1.36. Now we see that the *adjusted* difference in the mean tolerance scores is only .36, still highly significant but greatly reduced when we control for the other variables. The conclusion is that even when we control for things like region and education, there's still a difference (although much smaller) between the tolerance levels of urban and rural residents.

That's the most important result in the table, but the coefficients for the other variables are also interesting. People outside the South express significantly more racial tolerance than Southerners and, except for 1985, the regional difference is larger than the urban/ nonurban difference. In every year, more educated people express greater tolerance: Each additional year of schooling results in an increase of between .07 and .09 points in the tolerance index, depending on the year. Older people are less tolerant than younger people: Each year of age is associated with a decrease of .01 in the tolerance index. The coefficients of the other variables are either never statistically significant, or the results are inconsistent from one year to the next. There's little evidence here for an effect of sex, marital status, income, or children in the home.

A couple of other things are worth noting about this table. First, the R^2s range from .26 to .30, a fairly typical level for data of this sort. Second, unlike the two previous tables, this one reports neither the standard errors nor the t statistics. That's a fairly common way to save space but not a good one, in my opinion. Without standard errors or t statistics, it's impossible for the reader to calculate confidence intervals or exact p values.

2.4. What Determines How Much Time Married Couples Spend Together?

Kingston and Nock (1987) analyzed time diaries kept by 177 dual-earner married couples in 1981. Table 2.4 shows results of regressions in which the dependent variable is the number of minutes the couples spent together per day (excluding sleep time). There are two regression equations, one based on the husband's diary and the other based on the wife's diary. Most of the independent variables are self-explanatory, but two need some clarification. Off scheduling (minutes) is the total number of minutes per day in which one spouse is working while the other is not. Family prestige is an index based on both husband's and wife's occupation and education; it has a possible range from 0 to 100.

As with any statistical table, it's important to read the labels, legends, and footnotes carefully before trying to interpret the results. For example, unlike most tables in sociological journals, two stars after the coefficient mean that the p value is less than .10, not

TABLE 2.4 Regression of Minutes Together on Family Workday, Life Cycle, and Sociocultural Measures (*b*/standardized *b* in parentheses)

Independent Variables	Husband's Account	Wife's Account
Total minutes of work (husband + wife)	−0.151* (−0.239)	−0.115* (−0.187)
Off scheduling (minutes)	−0.190* (−0.309)	−.225* (−0.374)
Family income (1000s)	0.462 (0.043)	0.317 (0.030)
Family prestige	−1.447 (−0.102)	−2.148 (−0.156)
Respondent race (0 = nonwhite, 1 = white)	68.639 (0.072)	52.739 (0.057)
Number of children in household	−3.891 (−0.032)	−5.439 (−0.046)
Preschoolers? (0 = no, 1 = yes)	−7.959 (−0.022)	8.100 (0.023)
Years in present marriage	2.710** (0.159)	2.530** (0.152)
Constant	374.958	413.016
N	177	177
R^2	.213	.224
Significance (*p* value)	.000*	.000*

SOURCE: Table adapted from Kingston and Nock (1987). Reprinted by permission.
*$p < .05$; **$p < .10$.

.01. Many analysts would not even consider this to be statistically significant. Another difference is that the numbers in parentheses are not standard errors but standardized coefficients. If you missed this in the title, the fact that some of them are negative is a clear indication that they are not standard errors—standard errors can never be less than 0. Actually, the title is somewhat confusing because (*b*/standardized *b* in parentheses) does *not* mean that *b* is divided by standardized *b*. It simply means that the standardized coefficient lies immediately below the unstandardized coefficient in each case.

For both spouses, only two of the independent variables are statistically significant at the .05 level: total minutes of work and minutes of off scheduling. For the husband's report, each additional minute of total work time reduces the amount of time together by

.15 minutes. Each additional minute of off-schedule time reduces time together by .19 minutes. Based on the wife's report, the coefficient for total work time (–.12) is a little smaller in absolute value than the husband's, whereas the coefficient for off-schedule time (–.23) is a little larger. These small differences between husbands and wives are most likely due to random errors of one sort or another. There's some evidence that couples who've been married longer spend more time together, but the statistical significance of this result is debatable, at best.

It's not terribly surprising that work time and off-schedule time affect time couples spend together. What is surprising is that the other variables show little evidence of any effects. Most people would expect number of children and presence of a preschooler to have some impact. Actually, the coefficients for these variables are not all that small. Each additional child reduces the amount of time together by 4 to 5 minutes (depending on which spouse you listen to). Couples with a preschooler spend either 8 minutes less together (according to the husband) or 8 minutes more (according to the wife). Still, the fact that these coefficients are not statistically significant (even at the .10 level) means that we shouldn't put much stock in their values. There's also a whopping coefficient for race: White couples spend about an hour more together than nonwhite couples. Why isn't this statistically significant? Most likely because, according to the article, only 3% of the sample was nonwhite. That's only 5 couples out of 177, clearly not enough for a reliable comparison.

The last line in the table, labeled "Significance (p value)" is something we haven't seen before. It's the p value for testing the null hypothesis that *all* the coefficients are 0, sometimes referred to as a global test of significance. For both regressions, the p value is listed at .000. This doesn't mean that the p value is *exactly* 0, but it's 0 in the first three decimal places. In any case, a p value this small is statistically significant by anyone's criterion. We conclude, therefore, that the null hypothesis is false, and that *at least one* of the coefficients is not 0.

Why do we need this test, since we already have tests showing that some of the individual coefficients are not 0? When you're testing many coefficients for statistical significance, the p values for those tests can be misleading. If you have a 1 in 20 chance of being wrong on any one of those tests, the chance of making *at least* one mistake is substantially higher than that. The overall or global test can help protect you against such errors. A good rule of thumb is that if the global test is not significant, then you shouldn't put much stock in the individual tests.

As we've seen in previous tables, the "Constant" or intercept in these regressions is uninteresting. The R^2 of a little over .20 tells us that this set of independent variables accounts for only about 20% of the variation in time spent together.

2.5. Do Male Workers Dislike Working With Women?

Wharton and Baron (1987) studied a national sample of 822 male workers to see if those who worked in all-male job settings were happier about their jobs than those who worked in mixed-sex settings. There were three dependent variables:

- Job satisfaction: a scale based on responses to five questions, such as "All in all, how satisfied would you say you are with your job?" The possible scores ranged from 10 to 50, with a mean of 38.
- Job-related depression: a scale based on responses to four questions about how workers felt on the job, such as "I feel downhearted and blue." The possible scores ranged from 10 to 40, with a mean of 20.
- Job-related self-esteem: a four-item scale asking respondents how they saw themselves in their work: happy/sad, successful/not successful, important/not important, doing their best/not doing their best. Possible scores ranged from 10 to 70, with a mean of 60.

Based on their occupations, the male workers were classified into five different types of work settings:

- All male ($N = 416$)
- Mixed but segregated ($N = 131$)
- Predominantly male ($N = 196$)
- Mixed ($N = 59$)
- Predominantly female ($N = 20$)

A substantial majority of the men worked in settings where they had little or no direct contact with female employees.

How do we handle an independent variable with five categories? As explained in Section 1.2, the trick is to create a dummy variable for each of the categories, except for one category that is called the *reference category.* In this study, the reference category was All Male. One dummy variable was created for Mixed but Segregated so the 131 men who fell in this category got a 1 and everyone else got a 0. Another dummy variable was created for Predominantly Male: All 196 men in this category got a 1 and everyone else got a 0. Similar variables were created for Mixed and Predominantly Female.

Because workers and occupations differ in many ways besides sex composition, numerous other variables were included in the regressions as controls. Results for the three regressions are shown in Table 2.5. Notice that the sample size used for each regression is less than 700 even though the original sample had 822 men. That's because any man who had missing data on any of the independent variables was deleted from the sample. There are other ways of handling missing data, but this method (often called *listwise deletion*) is the simplest.

In the note at the bottom of the table, we are told that the coefficients are "metric," which is another way of saying that they are unstandardized rather than standardized. We also learn that a single asterisk means that a coefficient is significant at the .10 level, two asterisks mean significance at the .05 level, and three asterisks mean significant at the .01 level. The significance tests are said to be "two-tailed tests, except for effects pertaining to the mixed and predominantly male categories, which are one-tailed." You may recall from a previous statistics course that a one-tailed test is appropriate if you have a clear-cut expectation for the direction of the difference, whereas a two-tailed test is more appropriate if you have no such expectation. In this case, because the central hypothesis of the study was that men in mixed and predominantly male sex settings would be less happy with their jobs than men in all-male settings, the authors felt justified in choosing a one-tailed test. This is a more lenient test because the *p* value is obtained by dividing the two-tailed *p* value by 2. (Computer packages always give two-tailed *p* values.)

Our main interest is in the effects of the four dummy variables representing sex composition of the work setting. Whenever you have several dummy variables representing a single nominal variable, each coefficient is a comparison with the reference category, which, in this example, is the all-male setting. In the job satisfaction regression, we find a coefficient of –1.65 for predominantly male. This means that the average level of job satisfaction is about 1.65 points lower in predominantly male settings as compared with

TABLE 2.5 OLS Regression of Psychological Well-Being Variables on Gender Mix, Controlling for Individual, Job, and Organizational Characteristics

Independent Variables	Job Satisfaction (N = 696)	Job-Related Depression (N = 695)	Job-Related Self-Esteem (N = 692)
Mixed but segregated setting	.07	.40	.17
Predominantly male setting	−1.65**	1.30***	−1.95***
Mixed setting	−3.28**	1.59*	−3.09***
Predominantly female setting	.90	−2.01	.78
Race	.53	.86	.19
Age	.07	−.04	.07*
Age squared[a]	1.09E-03	−3.29E-03**	2.52E-04
High school graduate	−1.69	.34	−.84
Some college	−.46	.25	.39
College graduate	−.74	.55	−1.19
Unmarried	1.55	−1.11	.58
Married to housewife	3.70**	−1.90*	2.16
Lives in South	1.15	−.61	.85
Training time (SVP)	.55**	−.01	−.10
Danger	−2.27***	1.41***	−1.54**
Physical demands	.27	.16	.92**
Craft union	2.15*	.97	.35
Other union	.70	−.57	−.25
Job tenure	.26	.34	.05
Employer tenure	−.53	.13	.04
Steady	3.96***	.57	.69
Hours	−.03	.03	−.03
Organization scale	−.60***	.04	−.52***
Autonomy	.99**	−.14	1.43***
Authority	2.75***	−.61	2.76***
Log earnings	2.85***	−1.12*	1.78*
Log spouse earnings	.37**	−.15	.17
Status	.02	−9.71E-03	.02
R^2	.173	.072	.121
Adjusted R^2	.138	.033	.084
Standard error of estimate	9.304	5.727	9.269

SOURCE: Table adapted from Wharton and Baron (1987). Reprinted by permission.
NOTE: Metric coefficients are reported.
a. Squared deviation from average age in sample.
*$p \leq .10$; **$p \leq .05$; ***$p \leq .01$ (two-tailed tests, except for effects pertaining to the mixed and predominantly male categories, which are one-tailed).

all-male settings, controlling for other variables in the model. Similarly, the coefficient of –3.28 for mixed setting in the job satisfaction regression means that males working in mixed-sex settings average 3.28 points less on the job satisfaction scale than those working in all-male settings, controlling for other variables. These contrasts are statistically significant at the .05 level. On the other hand, job satisfaction in mixed but segregated settings and predominantly female settings are not significantly different from all-male settings. The results for these four variables are very similar in the job-related self-esteem regression.

There are also significant effects of predominantly male and mixed setting on job-related depression, but the coefficients have positive instead of negative signs. That's because higher values on the depression variable represent "worse" responses, whereas higher values on the satisfaction and self-esteem measures correspond to "better" responses. In all three regressions, the men in the predominantly female occupations are actually more positive about their job experiences than the men in the all-male settings, but the differences are not statistically significant, and it's plausible that the small number of men in these occupations may be a highly unusual group in other respects. In sum, the results seem to confirm the authors' hypothesis that men are happier when they don't have to work with women.

Although the results for the other variables are only incidental to the authors' main goal, we can learn something by examining them. Moving down the table, we see that race (1 = white, 0 = nonwhite) has little importance. Results for age are harder to interpret because "age squared" is also in the regression. This was done to allow for a possible nonlinear effect of age, a strategy we'll discuss in more detail in Chapter 8. The coefficients for the age squared term are reported in scientific notation: E-03 after a coefficient means that the decimal point should be moved three places to the left. The age squared term is not significant in the satisfaction and self-esteem regressions, indicating a lack of evidence for any departure from nonlinearity. This is one case where it would have been desirable to delete the nonsignificant variable from the regression to make the age effect more interpretable.

After the two age variables come three dummy variables representing education: high school graduate, some college, and college graduate. To interpret these coefficients, you have to know that the omitted category is "did not graduate from high school." Thus, the coefficient of –1.69 for high school graduate in the job satisfaction regression tells us that high school graduates have an average satisfaction score that's about 1.69 points lower than the average score for those who didn't graduate, controlling for other variables. None of the education coefficients is statistically significant, however.

Next come two dummy variables representing three categories of marital status. Here the omitted category is "married to an employed woman." We see that those married to a housewife are significantly more satisfied with their jobs than those whose wife works, and significantly less depressed on the job. Southern residence doesn't have any effect. Training time ("specific vocational preparation") has a positive impact on job satisfaction but not on depression or self-esteem. Jobs involving danger (a dummy variable) are rated substantially worse on all three scales. Jobs involving more physical work actually seem to enhance self-esteem on the job.

The two dummy variables for union membership represent a three-category nominal variable. The reference category is "not a union member." We see that members of craft unions report more satisfaction than nonunion workers, although the difference is only marginally significant. Years on the job (tenure) and years with the employer have little or no effect. Workers who say their job is "steady" are much more satisfied than other workers. Number of hours worked in the preceding week has little or no effect. Workers in large organizations (organizational scale) are less satisfied and have less self-esteem than those in smaller organizations. Those who report more authority and autonomy are more satisfied and have higher self-esteem.

Earnings seems to have a substantial impact on satisfaction and more modest effects on depression and self-esteem, but note that the variable is the *logarithm* of earnings. Entering the variable in this way forces earnings to have diminishing returns: each additional dollar of income has a smaller effect on the dependent variable. We'll discuss this in more detail in Chapter 8. Spouse earnings (again in logarithmic form) has a significant effect on job satisfaction but not on the other two dependent variables.

The R^2s at the bottom of the table indicate only modest predictive power for these regression models, ranging from a low of .072 to a high of .173. Below the R^2 is something we haven't seen before, called an adjusted R^2. The idea behind this adjustment is that regression models with lots of independent variables have a natural advantage over models with few independent variables in predicting the dependent variable. The adjusted R^2, explained more fully in Chapter 4, removes that advantage.

Just below that is the *standard error of the estimate*. This can be interpreted as the standard deviation of the dependent variable *after effects of the independent variables have been removed*. If we could perfectly predict the dependent variable from the set of independent variables (which would correspond to an R^2 of 1.0), the standard error of the estimate would be 0. On the other hand, when the R^2 is 0 (no predictive power), the standard error of the estimate is the same as the standard deviation of the dependent variable. This statistic is useful mainly in constructing confidence intervals around a predicted value of the dependent variable, which is largely irrelevant for this study. (It is not uncommon for journal articles to report statistics that are rather useless for the reader.)

Chapter Highlights

1. Asterisks after a regression coefficient usually indicate that the coefficient is significantly different from 0. The most common convention is one star for a p value below .05 and two stars for a p value below .01. This is not universal, however.

2. To interpret the numerical value of a regression coefficient, it's essential to understand the metrics of the dependent and independent variables.

3. Coefficients for dummy (0, 1) variables usually can be interpreted as differences in means on the dependent variable for the two categories of the independent variable, controlling for other variables in the regression model.

4. Standardized coefficients can be compared across independent variables with different units of measurement. They tell us how many standard deviations the dependent variable changes for an increase of one standard deviation in the independent variable.

5. The intercept (or constant) in a regression model rarely tells you anything interesting.

6. Don't exaggerate the importance of R^2 in evaluating a regression model. A model can still be worthwhile even if R^2 is low.

7. In computing a multiple regression, there is no distinction among different kinds of independent variables, nor do the results depend on the order which the variables appear in the model.

8. Varying the set of variables in the regression model can be helpful in understanding the causal relationships. If the coefficient for a variable x goes down when other variables are entered, it means that either (a) the other variables *mediate* the effect of x on the dependent variable y, or (b) the other variables affect both x and y and therefore the original coefficient of x was partly spurious.

9. If a dummy independent variable has nearly all the observations in one of its two categories, even large effects of this variable may not show up as statistically significant.

10. If the global F test for all the variables in a multiple regression model is not statistically significant, you should be very cautious about drawing any additional conclusions about the variables and their effects.

11. When multiple dummy variables are used to represent a categorical variable with more than two categories, it's crucial in interpreting the results to know which is the "omitted" category.

Questions to Think About

1. In a large organization, the average salary for men is $47,000 while the average salary for women is $30,000. A t test shows that this difference is significant at beyond the .001 level. When salary is regressed on years of work experience and a dummy variable for gender (male = 1, female = 0), the coefficient for sex is about $1,500 with a p value of .17. What would you conclude?

2. Dr. Smith regresses a measure of "happiness" on age, gender (male = 1, female = 0), and marital status (married = 1, unmarried = 0). All the coefficients are statistically significant at beyond the .05 level. Dr. Smith finds that the coefficient for gender is about five times as large as the coefficient for age. Can he legitimately conclude that gender is more important than age in predicting happiness? He also finds that the coefficient for gen-

TABLE 2.6 Regressions Predicting IQ Scores

	Model 1	Model 2
Brain size	.119*	.200**
	(.050)	(.066)
Gender (female = 1, male = 0)		−2.599
		(11.176)
Height (in.)		−2.767
		(1.447)
Weight (lbs.)		−.075
		(.220)
Constant	5.167	134.383
R^2	.13	.27
N	40	38

SOURCE: Table adapted from Willerman, Schultz, Rutledge, and Bigler (1987). Reprinted by permission.
NOTE: Standard errors are in parentheses.
*$p < .05$; **$p < .01$.

der is twice as large as the coefficient for marital status. What does this mean, if anything?

3. Hours per day spent watching TV is regressed on age (in years) and gender (female = 1, male = 0). The estimated intercept is 1.5. What does this number tell you, if anything?

4. The self-reported health study in Section 2.1 uses a dependent variable that is measured on a 5-point ordinal scale. Are there any potential problems with this?

The remaining questions pertain to the regression table shown as Table 2.6, based on data reported in Willerman, Schultz, Rutledge, and Bigler (1991). Brain size was measured by an MRI scan. It was a count of the number of "pixels" (smallest unit of uniform shading) in the scan.

5. What conclusions, if any, would you draw about the relationship between brain size and intelligence?

6. How would you interpret the coefficients for gender and weight in Model 2? Are these coefficients worth paying attention to? Why or why not?

7. What's the point of having two different models? What can we learn from comparing them?

8. Compute a t statistic for the height coefficient. Then find its p value.

9. Why does the constant (intercept) change so dramatically from Model 1 to Model 2?

10. Model 2 has a larger R^2 than Model 1. Does this mean it's a better model? Why or why not?

3 What Can Go Wrong With Multiple Regression?

Any tool as widely used as multiple regression is bound to be frequently *mis*used. Nowadays, statistical packages are so user-friendly that anyone can perform a multiple regression with a few mouse clicks. As a result, many researchers apply multiple regression to their data with little understanding of the underlying assumptions or the possible pitfalls. Although the review process for scientific journals is supposed to weed out papers with incorrect or misleading statistical methods, it often happens that the referees themselves have insufficient statistical expertise or are simply too rushed to catch the more subtle errors. The upshot is that you need to cast a critical eye on the results of any multiple regression, especially those you run yourself.

Fortunately, the questions that you need to ask are neither extremely technical nor large in number. They do require careful thought, however, which explains why even experts occasionally make mistakes or overlook the obvious. Virtually all the questions have to do with situations where multiple regression is used to make causal inferences. The requirements for a model used only for predictions are much less severe. I'll start with the more important questions and progress to those of lesser importance. Each question will be illustrated with examples drawn from Chapter 2.

3.1. Are Important Independent Variables Left Out of the Model?

In evaluating any regression model, it's just as important to think about what's *not* in the model as what's in it. There are two possible reasons for putting a variable in a regression model:

- You want to know the effect of the variable on the dependent variable
- You want to control for the variable

Obviously, researchers will include variables that are the main focus of their study, but they may not be so careful about including important control variables. (Remember that the multiple regression model makes no distinction between the study variables and the control variables.)

What makes a control variable important? To answer this question, you need to answer two other questions:

- Does the variable have a causal effect on the dependent variable?
- Is the variable *correlated* with those variables whose effects are the focus of the study?

For a control variable to be considered important, the answers to both questions must be "yes." If it has a strong effect on the dependent variable but is unrelated to the independent variables already in the model, there's no need to include it. That's why multiple regression is not essential for most randomized experiments—the randomization process is designed to remove any correlation between the treatment variable and the characteristics of the individuals in the study. Similarly, a potential control variable may be highly correlated with one of the independent variables in the regression model, but if it has no impact on the dependent variable, it can safely be omitted.

What happens when an important control variable is omitted? In the language of statisticians, what happens is *bias*. Simply put, bias means that the estimates of the regression coefficients for variables in the model tend to be either too high or too low. If the bias is large enough, we may conclude that a variable has an effect on the dependent variable when it really doesn't, or we could conclude that it doesn't have an effect when it really does. In the language of social scientists, the conclusions are *spurious*.

These are all matters of degree. If the effect of the omitted variable on the dependent variable is small, then the bias will be small. If the correlation between the omitted variable and the included variable is small, the bias will also be small. The bias is also concentrated in the coefficients for those variables that are correlated with the omitted variable. Here's an example. Suppose you regress income (the dependent variable) on years of schooling and age, as in Chapter 1, and you find a large effect of schooling. A critic might say, "The schooling effect is biased because you didn't control for intelligence. Intelligent people spend more years in school and they also earn more money." On the other hand, we wouldn't expect much bias in the age coefficient because there's little correlation between IQ measures and age.

Now let's consider two of the examples in Chapter 2. Table 2.3 purports to show that living in cities makes people more racially tolerant. After controlling for several other variables, people in larger cities still had higher tolerance scores than those in smaller cities or rural areas. But were all the relevant variables included? Specifically, did the regression model omit any variables that are associated with both tolerance and urban residence? Religion is one possibility. It is well known that Jews tend to be concentrated in urban areas, and there is also a long history of Jewish alliance with organizations promoting racial equality. Perhaps if the regression model included a dummy variable for whether or not the respondent was Jewish, the coefficient for urbanism would no longer be statistically significant. My own guess is that the proportion of Jews in the United States is sufficiently small (only about 3%) that putting this variable in the model would not make a major difference, but you never know for sure until you try.

Table 2.2 is also problematic. In this regression, the author wanted to test the hypothesis that mental patients who believed that most people discriminate against mental patients would be more demoralized. He found a significant coefficient for devaluation-discrimination controlling for four variables: marital status, ethnicity (Hispanics vs. others), hospitalization, and diagnosis (schizophrenia vs. depression). He also reported that three other variables—sex, years of education, and employment status—were originally in the regression equation but were deleted because they were not statistically significant. Again, this is consistent with the principle that you can omit variables if they have no effect on the dependent variable.

Unfortunately, it's not all that difficult to think of other variables that might affect both discrimination beliefs and demoralization. One obvious possibility is actual *experience* of discrimination. Some of these mental patients may have been treated much worse than other patients—by family, friends, coworkers, or mental health practitioners. It wouldn't be surprising if they were more demoralized and also believed more strongly that people discriminated against mental patients. Another possibility is seriousness of illness, which is likely to affect both beliefs and demoralization. The author might claim that he controlled for seriousness by including hospitalization and diagnosis, but these are very crude proxies. I would expect considerable variation in seriousness of illness among hospitalized patients or among schizophrenics. Finally, there are many standard sociodemographic variables, such as age and income, that could affect both variables. In the light of these possibilities, I'm far from convinced that beliefs about discrimination have a causal impact on demoralization.

When you have a clear idea about how a particular omitted variable is related to the dependent variable and an included independent variable, you can often make a reasonable guess about the direction of the bias. For example, as a mental illness becomes more serious, we would expect a patient to become more demoralized and to have stronger beliefs of discrimination. That would produce a spuriously *positive* relationship between those two variables. If this argument is correct, the coefficient for devaluation-discrimination in Table 2.2 is probably an overestimate of the true coefficient.

3.2. Does the Dependent Variable Affect Any of the Independent Variables?

When we estimate a regression model, we often interpret the coefficients as measuring the causal effects of the independent variables on the dependent variable. But what if the "dependent" variable actually affects one or more of the "independent" variables? If it does, the resulting biases can be every bit as serious as those produced by the omission of important variables. This problem— known as *reverse causation*—actually can be worse than the omitted variables problem because

- Every coefficient in the regression model may be biased
- It's hard to design a study that will adequately solve this problem

Unfortunately, there's rarely any information in the data that can help you determine the direction of causation. Instead, decisions about the direction of causation have to be based almost entirely on your knowledge of the phenomenon you're studying. There are, in fact, several different ways to argue against the possibility of reverse causation. If the data come from a randomized experiment, then randomization assures us that the dependent variable isn't influencing who gets the treatment. Often, the time ordering of the variables gives us a pretty clear indication of the causal direction. For example, we usually feel safe in supposing that parents' educational attainment affects the educational attainment of their adult children, not the other way around. Even when there's no time ordering, our knowledge of basic physical and biological processes sometimes gives us a pretty good idea of the causal direction. We feel confident, for example, that a man's height might affect his social prestige, but social prestige couldn't affect height.

With non-experimental data, most applications of regression analysis involve some ambiguity about the direction of causality. In such cases, the causal mechanism could run in either direction, perhaps in both. Equation 2 of Table 2.1 includes "unable to work" as a predictor of self-rated health, but the predominant reason for inability to work is poor health, so the inclusion of this variable could potentially bias other coefficients in the model. It would have been preferable to remove people who were unable to work from the data set before running this regression.

The regression in Table 2.2 is also vulnerable to this criticism. The model presumes that beliefs about discrimination and devaluation affect the demoralization of mental patients, but isn't it equally plausible that demoralized patients are more likely to believe that mental patients are discriminated against? If so, then the coefficient for devaluation-discrimination in Table 2.2 could be highly biased.

Things are somewhat less ambiguous with the urbanism regression reported in Table 2.3. The core hypothesis is that living in a large urban area promotes racial tolerance. That certainly makes sense. One could also argue, however, that more racially tolerant people are more likely to move from non-urban to urban areas and that racially *in*tolerant people are more likely to move from urban to non-urban areas, thereby producing a relationship between urbanism and tolerance. Under this scenario, tolerance causes urbanism. One way to reduce the ambiguity is to focus on residence at age 16 rather than in adulthood, when the questionnaire was administered.

At age 16, people haven't yet had the opportunity to move to places that are more consistent with their attitudes. In fact, tables presented in the original article show that people living in urban areas at age 16 are more racially tolerant in adulthood that those living in non-urban areas at age 16, thereby increasing our confidence that urbanism causes tolerance rather than the reverse.

Table 2.4 purports to show that married couples spend more time together each day if they (a) work fewer hours, (b) work on the same schedule, and (c) have been married longer. What's the direction of causality here? In this case, as in many others, it's helpful to think about how people typically make decisions. Most people are very constrained with respect to the number of hours they work and the scheduling of those hours. Once those constraints are set, they then make decisions about how to spend their time away from work. This reasoning supports the causal ordering assumed by Table 2.4. On the other hand, there are undoubtedly some couples who choose their jobs or their job schedules to accommodate their desires to spend more (or less) time together. So there's still some ambiguity about the causal ordering. This is also true for the apparent effect of length of marriage on time spent together. Maybe it's the other way around: Perhaps couples who spend more time together stay married longer.

In the final example, Table 2.5, we find that the sex composition of occupations appears to affect men's job satisfaction, job-related depression, and job-related self-esteem. In this case, the direction of causality seems relatively unambiguous. If anything, I would expect that men with higher self-esteem are more willing to enter mixed occupations because they feel more confident in less traditional settings, but that would run contrary to the observed results.

It should be clear from these examples that most applications of multiple regression involve some uncertainty about the direction of causality. As with omitted variables, the issue here is one of degree. If we can make an equally persuasive argument for x causing y and for y causing x, then we must be very wary about interpreting a regression with y as the dependent variable and x as the independent variable. On the other hand, if we have a compelling argument for x affecting y but only a weak or contrived argument for y causing x, then we can feel much more secure about interpreting the regression of y on x. Even then, however, some uncertainty usually remains.

3.3. How Well Are the Independent Variables Measured?

As we've repeatedly seen, to control for a variable in a multiple regression, you have to measure that variable and include it in the model. But it's not enough simply to measure a variable—you have to measure it well. To the degree that a variable is afflicted with measurement error, the coefficients for that variable and other variables will be biased. I already hinted at this problem when I discussed Table 2.2, showing the relationship between demoralization and beliefs of discrimination among mental patients. I said that both variables could be affected by seriousness of the illness, which could produce a spurious relationship between them. Two variables in the model—hospitalization and diagnosis—could be taken as measures of seriousness, but only crude measures at best. Within each category of these two variables, there was undoubtedly much variation in seriousness. More generally, whenever an independent variable is measured with error, we can say that for each measured value of that variable, there may be many different values of the true variable. Consequently, the measured variable does not fully control for the true variable.

In a regression with a single independent variable, measurement error in that variable will tend to bias its coefficient toward zero. In models with more than one independent variable, the biases are harder to predict. Usually, however, the coefficients for the variables with a greater degree of measurement error tend to be underestimated (closer to zero), whereas the coefficients for the variables with less measurement error tend to be overestimated (further from zero).

For Equation 1 of Table 2.1, measurement error is not likely to be a serious problem. We can usually do a pretty good job of getting accurate information on years of schooling, sex, race, age, and marital status. However, questions could be raised about the marital status variable, which is a simple dichotomy of married vs. unmarried. Obviously, the unmarried category could be further decomposed into never married, divorced, and widowed. If there are substantial differences in the dependent variable (self-rated health) across these three subcategories, then marital status has not been adequately controlled.

Measurement error is potentially more serious in the study of mental patients (Table 2.2). I already discussed the inadequacy of hospitalization as a measure of seriousness. We can also raise questions about the key independent variable, the 12-item scale measuring beliefs about discrimination and devaluation. "Soft" measures like this one should always be scrutinized for possible measurement error. In defense of the scale, the author reports that it has an estimated *reliability* of .78. Reliability is a number between 0 and 1 that quantifies the degree of measurement error in a variable. The value of .78 tells us that 78% of the variance of this variable is "true" variance and the other 22% of the variance is measurement error. This is OK by most social science standards, but not terrific. If this were the only independent variable in the model, its coefficient would be underestimated by about 22%. This would bias the results *against* the author's hypothesis, so the fact that he *does* find an effect of this variable cannot be explained away by measurement error.

Estimates of reliability are valuable indications of the degree of measurement error, but you should never accept them as absolute truth. First, there are many different ways to estimate reliability, and different methods can produce markedly different answers. Second, conventional methods for estimating reliability tell us only about the *stability* of the variable in question, not how well it measures what we really want it to measure. Self-reports of age, for example, are highly reliable in the sense that people tend to give consistent answers if you ask them their age more than once, but most people would be highly skeptical of a study that used self-reported age as a measure of political conservatism. In short, we need to be concerned about the *validity* of our measurements, not just their reliability. Unfortunately, validity is a much more difficult notion to quantify, both in theory and in practice.

For a final example of measurement error, let's consider the study of gender segregation on the job (Table 2.5). Men were divided into five groups according to how much gender segregation they experienced at work. As the authors admit, "our sample permitted only indirect measurement of the gender mix in each respondent's work setting" (Wharton & Baron, 1987, p. 578). What this means is that they used census data on proportions of workers who were male and female for jobs of that particular type in that particular industry. Thus, they didn't know the actual degree of gender segregation experienced by each man in the sample. As a result, the coefficients they estimated for the various gender categories are probably smaller than if they had actually interviewed each man and asked him about the number of his coworkers who were men and women. Because the coefficients were still statistically significant, the evidence clearly supports the authors' hypotheses.

3.4. Is the Sample Large Enough to Detect Important Effects?

Sample size has a profound effect on tests of statistical significance. With a sample of 60 people, a correlation has to be at least .25 (in magnitude) to be significantly different from zero (at the .05 level). With a sample of 10,000 people, any correlation larger than .02 will be statistically significant. The reason is simple: There's very little information in a small sample, so estimates of correlations are very unreliable. If we get a correlation of .20, there may still be a good chance that the true correlation is zero. Similarly, large samples contain lots of information that allows us to estimate the correlation very precisely. Even if we get a correlation of only .04 in a sample of 10,000, the chances are slim that the true correlation is zero. This means that you should always keep sample size in mind when you're looking at the results of significance tests.

Let's first look at the problem of interpreting results from small samples. In Table 2.4, we saw that most of the independent variables were not significant predictors of the time that married couples spend together. For example, the coefficient for race was not significant, even though it was rather large. Are we justified, then, in concluding that there are no racial differences in the time couples spend together? Absolutely not. The sample consists of 177 couples, only five of which were nonwhite. Although this is not an extremely small sample, neither is it very large. It's quite possible that a sample of 1,000 cases would have provided clear evidence for a race difference. In the absence of such a sample, however, we just don't know whether race matters or not. The general principle is this: In a small sample, statistically significant coefficients should be taken seriously, but a nonsignificant coefficient is extremely weak evidence for the absence of an effect.

Statisticians often describe small samples as having *low power* to test hypotheses. There is another, entirely different problem with small samples that is frequently confused with the issue of power. Most of the test statistics that researchers use (such as *t* tests, *F* tests, and chi-square tests) are only approximations. These approximations are usually quite good when the sample is large but may deteriorate markedly when the sample is small. That means that p values calculated for small samples may be only rough approximations of the true p values. If the calculated p value is .02, the true value might be something like .08. In multiple regression, the p values are exact *if* the data satisfy certain demanding distributional assumptions (Chapter 6). That's a big "if," however, and in all other cases the statistics are only approximations.

Although these two problems—low power and poor approximations of test statistics—are entirely distinct, they sometimes become intertwined in practice in an unfortunate way. Because it's difficult to get statistically significant results in small samples, regression analysts are often tempted to raise the level of p values that they will accept as statistically significant, say from .05 to .10. But because the p values themselves may be poor approximations in small samples, I would argue for exactly the opposite approach. Instead of requiring a p value less than .05 for statistical significance, I think a good case can be made for a criterion closer to .01 to allow for the possibility that the p value is underestimated.

That brings us to the inevitable question: What's a big sample and what's a small sample? As you may have guessed, there's no clear-cut dividing line. Almost anyone would consider a sample less than 60 to be small, and virtually everyone would agree that a sample of 1,000 or more is large. In between, it depends on a lot of factors that are difficult to quantify, at least in practice.

3.5. Is the Sample So Large That Trivial Effects Are Statistically Significant?

In theory, a bigger sample is always better. With a large sample, you don't have to worry that the p values are only approximations, and bigger samples give you more precise estimates of the coefficients. What can be bad about that? In practice, however, large samples can sometimes lead to incorrect conclusions.

In any scientific investigation, there are bound to be some sources of bias. Perhaps the sample wasn't quite random, or maybe the respondents tended to overestimate their income. We do everything we can to minimize those biases, but we can never eliminate them entirely. Consequently, small, artifactual relationships are likely to creep into the data. A large sample is like a very sensitive measuring instrument. It's so sensitive that it detects these artifactual relationships along with the true relationships.

The essence of the problem, then, is that with very large samples, almost any variable you put in a regression model is likely to show up as statistically significant, even if it has no real effect. When a variable has a statistically significant coefficient, we say that its coefficient is unlikely to be zero. In a large sample, the coefficient may be so small that it's not worth serious attention.

In practice, this means that when a regression is run on a large sample, it's not enough to say that a coefficient is statistically significant. You must also determine whether it is *substantively* significant. That is, you must look carefully at the magnitude of the coefficient to see if it is large enough to have theoretical or practical importance.

Suppose, for example, that you run a regression with 10,000 adults in which the dependent variable is annual income (in dollars) and one of the independent variables is a dummy variable for gender, coded 1 for male and 0 for female. You find that the gender coefficient is positive and statistically significant at the .05 level. "Aha!" you say, "This is evidence for sex discrimination." Maybe so, but what if the coefficient is only 45.2, indicating that men, on average, make $45 a year more than women? Although there may be some people who would take this seriously, I can't imagine a reasonable person getting either upset with or intrigued by a difference that small.

In this example, income and gender are such familiar variables that it's fairly easy to get a sense of the substantive significance of the coefficients. However, with many of the variables used in social science research, the metrics are so unfamiliar that it's hard to get a clear notion of what's a big coefficient and what's small. In these situations, standardized coefficients—when available—can be helpful. As we've already seen, standardized coefficients do not depend on the metrics of the variables and therefore can be used to gauge the relative importance of different variables. If a standardized coefficient is very small, say less than .05, it tells us that the variable explains very little of the variation in the dependent variable, even though it may be statistically significant.

In the examples considered in Chapter 2, the largest sample (2,031 cases) was used for the self-reported health regression (Table 2.1). Many of the variables in this table had coefficients with p values less than .001, reflecting the large size of the sample. Should we take all these effects seriously? Consider the coefficient for marital status, which has a p value less than .01 in Equation 1. Although statistically significant, the difference between married and unmarried people is only about 0.1 on the 5-point scale of self-reported health. This does not seem like a very large effect. The standardized coefficient is only .058, which is pretty low as these things go, so it would probably be unwise to make a big deal out of the effect of marital status on self-rated health.

3.6. Do Some Variables Mediate the Effects of Other Variables?

Does socioeconomic status (SES) affect SAT scores? That seems reasonable. But suppose you run a regression model for a sample of college freshmen with SAT score as the dependent variable and SES and high school GPA as the independent variables. You find that the coefficient for GPA is highly significant but the coefficient for SES is not significant. Are you justified in concluding that SES has no effect on SAT scores? We already saw in Section 3.4 that if the sample is too small, a nonsignificant coefficient is not a sufficient reason for concluding that a variable has no effect on the dependent variable. Even if the sample is not small, there is another reason for being cautious in concluding that a variable has no effect: It's possible that other variables *mediate* the effect of that variable. If those other variables are also included in the regression model, the effect of the variable you're interested in may disappear.

In our hypothetical example, let's suppose that SES has a big effect on GPA, and GPA, in turn, has a big effect on SAT scores. We can represent this by a simple *path diagram*:

$$\text{SES} \rightarrow \text{GPA} \rightarrow \text{SAT}.$$

If this causal structure is correct, then it's appropriate to say that SES affects SAT scores because improving people's SES results in an increase in their SAT scores. But the effect is *indirect*, through improvements in high school scholastic achievement (GPA). We may also say that GPA is an *intervening* variable between SES and SAT. If we put both independent variables in the regression model, the overall effect of SES on SAT is obscured. We may mistakenly conclude that SES has no impact on SAT scores when it may actually be quite important.

The point is *not* that the regression of SAT on both GPA and SES is wrong; rather, the point is that any regression model only estimates the *direct* effect of each variable, controlling for all the other variables in the model. In our example, the direct effect of SES can be interpreted as its effect on SAT scores that *does not* operate through GPA. The regression doesn't tell you anything, however, about possible indirect effects. In many cases, these indirect effects may be of great interest.

How can you tell if a variable has important indirect effects? First, you need to have some clear notion of the causal ordering of the variables in the regression model. In our example, it's apparent that SES affects GPA rather than the reverse. Second, you need more information than you can get from just a single regression model. There are two ways to get this information, but I'll discuss only one of them here. In our example, if we remove GPA from the regression model, then the coefficient for SES is its *total effect* on SAT scores. In general,

Total Effect = Direct Effect + Indirect Effects.

Because we already have an estimate of the direct effect from the regression of SAT on both SES and GPA, we can calculate the indirect effect by subtracting the direct effect from the total effect. Suppose, for example, that when we regress SAT score on SES alone, the coefficient is 15 (that is, each one-unit increase in SES yields a 15-point increase in SAT score). When we regress SAT score on *both* SES and GPA, the coefficient of SAT declines to 5. Then the direct effect of SES is 5, and the indirect effect (through GPA) is 10.

The general principle is this: If you're interested in the effect of x on y, but there are other variables w and z that may mediate that effect, estimate the regression twice, both with and without the intervening variables w and z. The coefficient of x in the regression without w and z is the total effect of x. The difference in the two coefficients for x represents the indirect effects of x through w and z. Of course, if all you have are published regression results, you may not be able to do these calculations.

A couple of additional points should be keep in mind. First, the inclusion of an intervening variable in a regression model doesn't always eliminate the effect of the variable of interest. If the variable

of interest also has a direct effect, then the inclusion of the intervening variable may only reduce its coefficient, not eliminate it. Second,
for any causal relationship, it's nearly always possible to think of
one or more intervening variables. Thus, what we call a direct effect
in one model can potentially be converted into an indirect effect if
we add mediating variables.

Knowledge of intervening variables is usually a crucial part of
understanding how a causal process works. It's nice to know, for
instance, that people in urban areas are more racially tolerant (Table
2.3). But why are they more tolerant? Is it because they have more
face-to-face contact with people of different races? Or is it because
teachers in urban schools put more stress on racial tolerance? The
way to tell is to actually measure these variables and put them in
the regression model. If the coefficient for urbanism goes down
substantially, that's evidence that these variables mediate the urbanism effect.

Do mediating variables create any problems for the interpretation of the examples in Chapter 2? In the self-rated health regression
(Table 2.1), the search for variables mediating the effect of education
was a major aim of the study. To accomplish this goal, models were
estimated both with and without the potential mediating variables
to see how the coefficient for education changed. For the mental
patient study (Table 2.2), it seems implausible that patients' beliefs
about devaluation and discrimination could affect control variables
like diagnosis, hospitalization, and so on, so there's not much cause
for concern here. With the urbanism study (Table 2.3), there's a
possibility that urban residence could be affecting education (which
has a strong affect on tolerance) and income (which has a modest
effect in two of the years). Hence, part of the effect of urban residence
could be indirect, through income and education.

3.7. Are Some Independent Variables
Too Highly Correlated?

I've encountered several people with the mistaken notion that
the independent variables in a regression analysis should not be
correlated with each other. I'm not sure where they got this idea—
maybe because they're called *independent* variables. As we saw in
Section 3.1, if the independent variables are all uncorrelated, you

don't even need multiple regression: Two-variable regressions or simple correlations are sufficient.

Multiple regression is designed precisely for separating the effects of two or more independent variables on a dependent variable when the independent variables are correlated with one another, but there's a limit to what regression can do. Imagine that you have a sample of AIDS patients and you want to study what factors affect their survival time. You're particularly interested in homosexual orientation (1 = yes, 0 = no) and intravenous drug use (1 = yes, 0 = no). You find that in your sample all the IV drug users are heterosexual and all the nonusers are homosexual. Sorry, but you're out of luck. There's no way you can get separate estimates of the effects of these two variables on survival time, either with multiple regression or with any other statistical method.

This problem goes by the name of *multicollinearity*, and what we've just seen is an extreme case where the two variables are perfectly correlated. If you tried to put both these variables into a regression program, either you would get an error message or the program would kick one variable or the other out of the model.

Multicollinearity doesn't have to be so extreme to cause problems, and, unfortunately, those problems often go undetected. Suppose that in the AIDS example, there were two homosexual IV drug users out of 1,000 patients. The correlation isn't perfect anymore, so you could do the regression and you'd get results. Would the numbers mean anything? Not likely. What would happen is that the estimated standard errors for the regression coefficients would be very large, accurately reflecting the fact that you can't get very precise estimates of the effect of each variable controlling for the other variable. With large standard errors, it's unlikely that either coefficient would be statistically significant. On the other hand, it's entirely possible that if we ran the regression with only the IV drug use variable or, alternatively, only the homosexuality variable, we might find large and highly significant coefficients for both variables. This would tell us that one or both of these variables had a substantial effect on survival time, but we couldn't say which one. If we ran only the model that included both variables, we would incorrectly conclude that *neither* variable had any effect on survival time.

Multicollinearity has other effects, but this one is the most worrisome—the possibility of concluding that two variables have no effect when one or the other of them actually has a strong effect. How highly correlated do two (or more) variables have to be before multicollinearity becomes a problem? That's a fairly technical issue that I'm going to postpone until Chapter 7. You almost certainly have problems if the correlation is above .80, but there may be difficulties that appear well below that value.

Is multicollinearity a problem for any of the examples in Chapter 2? We can't be sure because the authors don't report the correlations among the independent variables. Just examining the variables, I would be surprised if any of them were so highly correlated as to cause errors in interpretation. One possible exception is in the example of marital time. Two of the variables in the regression model are number of children and presence of preschoolers. I would expect these variables to have a correlation of perhaps .50 and possibly larger. The fact that neither of them has a statistically significant coefficient could be a consequence of multicollinearity.

3.8. Is the Sample Biased?

This question needs to be asked for *any* statistical analysis, regardless of the method. There are actually two aspects to this question, however, relating to the notions of *internal* and *external validity*.

With respect to external validity, the question is whether the results for the sample can be generalized to other groups or populations of interest. If the regression is estimated with a simple random sample from some well-defined population, then you are in a good position to generalize from the sample to the population. If the sample is a probability sample but not a simple random sample, the regression may require weighting of some sort, although this is a controversial issue. The study of self-rated health in Section 2.1, the study of urbanism in Section 2.3, and the study of male workers in Section 2.5 were all based on probability samples of the adult U.S. population; this gives us some confidence in the generalizability of the conclusions.

If the sample is merely a convenience sample, then you need to think carefully about whether causal relationships that hold in the sample are likely to hold in other groups in which you may be interested. In the study of mental patients (Section 2.2), the sample was drawn entirely from

outpatient clinics and inpatient clinics in the same general area [Washington Heights] of New York City. The goal was to select patients in two diagnostic categories, major depression and schizophrenia and schizophrenic-like psychiatric disorders. In addition, considerable effort was made to locate cases in their first episode of each of these types of disorders. (Link, 1987, pp. 100-101)

This is clearly not a probability sample: It is restricted to a specific geographic area, and it apparently involved a substantial amount of recruitment effort on the part of the research team. That should raise a number of questions about the generalizability of the results. Are mental patients in this section of New York City likely to be different with respect to the variables or relationships in this study from patients in other geographical areas? How were the clinics selected? Was there a substantial rate of refusal? Answers to these questions could raise doubts about how well the results of this study apply to other situations.

Leaving aside the question of whether the results for the sample apply to other groups as well, we must also consider internal validity—whether the sample selection process can produce erroneous or misleading results for the sample itself. Again, this is usually not a major concern if the sample is a probability sample from some well-defined population, and if the nonresponse rate is low. It should be a concern, however, for convenience samples, or when a high proportion of potential respondents refuse to cooperate or can't be located. Imagine a study of the relationship between education and income in which people who were inconsistent on these two variables tended not to respond to the survey. That is, what if people with high education and low income, or low education and high income, were disproportionately less likely to return the questionnaire? Such a differential response pattern could easily produce an apparent correlation between education and income when there was really no relationship. In most applications, we don't expect such differential response patterns, but that doesn't mean that they don't occur.

3.9. Are There Any Other Problems to Watch For?

The preceding eight problems are the ones I believe most often lead to serious errors in judging the results of a multiple regression. By no means do they exhaust the possible pitfalls that may arise. Before concluding this chapter, I'll briefly mention a few others.

Some problems are implicit in the essential features of multiple regression that I discussed in Chapter 1. For example, the regression model assumes that the relationships are all linear. What if they're not? Modest departures from linearity are unlikely to cause really serious inferential errors. The linear model is usually a reasonably good approximation to a wide range of mathematical forms. If the relationship is highly nonlinear, however, we can sometimes be led astray. It may be, for instance, that punishment reduces deviant behavior up to a certain point, but if the punishment becomes too severe, deviant behavior may increase. If we apply a strictly linear model to the data, the positive and negative effects of deviance may cancel out, leaving us with no apparent relationship. Ways of extending the linear model to account for such *curvilinear* relationships will be discussed in Chapter 8.

Also in Chapter 1, we saw that variables measured on an ordinal scale are not strictly appropriate for multiple regression, even though many researchers use them anyway. Most of the time this practice is innocuous, but it can occasionally lead to errors or misinterpretations. The problem is actually quite similar to the discussion of inadequate measurement in Section 3.3. If we want to control for intelligence, for example, but we only have a crude ranking of intelligence, then our statistical control may not be very effective. As a result, we may be led to erroneous conclusions.

I'll mention one last problem that, unfortunately, is very hard to evaluate from published regression results. It sometimes happens that regression results are very strongly influenced by a small number of cases in the sample. These influential cases are usually those that have extreme values on either the independent or the dependent variables. There are graphical and numerical methods for detecting influential observations. One simple approach is to delete them from the analysis and see how much difference it makes. If regression results are highly sensitive to the presence or absence of a few influential cases, then we should be less confident in our results.

Chapter Highlights

1. Leaving important variables out of a regression model can bias the coefficients of other variables and lead to spurious conclusions.

2. Important variables are those that affect the dependent variable and are correlated with the variables that are the focus of the study.

3. If the dependent variable in a regression model has an effect on one or more independent variables, any or all of the regression coefficients may be seriously biased.

4. Non-experimental data rarely tell you anything about the direction of a causal relationship. You must decide the direction based on your prior knowledge of the phenomenon you're studying.

5. Time ordering usually gives us the most important clues about the direction of causality.

6. Measurement error in independent variables leads to bias in the coefficients. Variables with more measurement error tend to have coefficients that are biased toward 0. Variables with little or no measurement error tend to have coefficients that are biased away from 0.

7. The degree of measurement error in a variable is usually quantified by an estimate of its reliability, a number between 0 and 1. A reliability of 1 indicates that the variable is perfectly measured; a reliability of 0 indicates that the variation in the variable is pure measurement error.

8. With small samples, even large regression coefficients may not be statistically significant. In such cases, you are *not* justified in concluding that the variable has no effect—the sample may not have been large enough to detect it.

9. In small samples, the approximations used to calculate p values may not be very accurate, so be cautious in interpreting them.

10. In large samples, even trivial effects may be statistically significant. You need to look carefully at the magnitude of each coefficient to determine whether it is large enough to be substantively interesting. When the measurement scale of the variable is unfamiliar, standardized coefficients can be helpful in evaluating the substantive significance of a regression coefficient.

11. If you're interested in the effect of x on y, but the regression model also includes intervening (mediating) variables w and z, the coefficient for x may be misleadingly small. You have estimated the direct effect of x on y, but you have missed the indirect effects through w and z.

12. If intervening variables w and z are deleted from the regression model, the coefficient for x represents its total effect on y. The total effect is the sum of the direct and indirect effects.

13. If two or more independent variables are highly correlated, it's difficult to get good estimates of the effect of each variable controlling for the others. This problem is known as multicollinearity.

14. When two independent variables are highly collinear, it's easy to incorrectly conclude that neither has an effect on the dependent variable.

15. As with any statistical analysis, it's important to consider whether the sample is representative of the intended population. A probability sample is the best way to get a representative sample.

16. If a substantial portion of the intended sample refuses to participate in the study, regression analysis may produce biased estimates.

Questions to Think About

1. Dr. Johnson wants to see if job satisfaction is affected by salary. For a sample of workers in a large corporation, she regresses a measure of job satisfaction on salary, years of schooling, and age. What variables are omitted that might produce bias in the coefficient for salary? (Consider both characteristics of the job and characteristics of the employee.)

2. A psychologist hypothesizes that sleep deprivation is a cause of depression. For a sample of college students, he regresses a measure of depression on hours of sleep in the previous week, plus a large number of control variables. He finds that, as expected, those who get less sleep are more depressed. Can he reasonably conclude the sleep loss causes depression? Why or why not?

3. A criminologist finds that, among college students, there is a strong correlation between frequency of cigarette smoking and frequency of alcohol use. In a regression model, which of these should be the dependent variable and which should be the independent variable?

4. A college admissions director finds that there is a modest correlation between SAT scores prior to admission and GPA at the time of graduation. In a regression model, which of these should be the dependent variable and which should be the independent variable?

5. For the study on sleep and depression described in question 2, the researcher is concerned that both sleep loss and depression may be caused by the level of external stress, leading to a spurious relationship. To control for stress, he asks students "On a scale of 1 to 10, how much stress do you experience in your life?" with 10 being a high level of stress and 1 being very little. When the stress rating is included in the regression model, there is still a significant effect of sleep on depression. Do you see any problems with this procedure?

6. A medical researcher wants to see if zinc lozenges reduce the severity of colds. For a sample of 20 volunteers with colds, she randomly assigns 10 to get the zinc lozenges and 10 to get a placebo. She examines several outcome measures but finds no significant differences between the two groups. Is she justified in concluding that the lozenges are ineffective? Why or why not?

7. For a national probability sample of 15,000 high school seniors seeking college admission, a regression is performed with SAT scores as the dependent variable. There are many independent variables, including an IQ measure, parental income, and a dummy variable for public (0) versus private (1) high school. The coefficient for the dummy variable is positive and statistically significant, with a p value of .001. Is it correct to conclude that private schools do a better job of educating students? Why or why not? What else should be checked?

8. A baseball team statistician wants to know if his team has an advantage in playing home games. He does a regression in which the units of analysis are all the games played by his team in the last season and the dependent variable is number of points scored by his team. Independent variables include a home/away dummy variable, number of hits in the game by his team, number of strikeouts by his team's pitcher, and the season batting average of the opposing team. The home/away dummy does not have a statistically significant effect. Do you see any problems with this analysis?

9. A survey of computer users asks them "On a scale of 1 to 10, how much do you enjoy working with your computer?" This is the dependent variable in a regression analysis. One of the independent variables is machine type (1 = IBM compatible, 0 = Macintosh or compatible). Another independent variable is system software (1 = Microsoft product, 0 = any other software company). Is there a problem here?

4 How Do I Run a Multiple Regression?

Everything so far in this book has been designed to teach you how to read, interpret, and critique the results of multiple regression done by *other* people. If you're reading this chapter, I assume that the time has come for you to run a multiple regression of your own. Great! You can never fully understand or appreciate a technique until you've tried it yourself.

Doing a multiple regression is easy. Doing it *right* is another matter. This chapter deals mostly with the easy part, the mechanics of telling a computer what to do. The hard part is the careful thinking that needs to be done *before* you fire up the computer. Chapter 3 should help you with that part.

4.1. How Do I Choose a Computer Package?

Bivariate regression—with one dependent variable and one independent variable—is easily done on a hand calculator if the sample size is small. In fact, many hand calculators have built-in bivariate regression functions. For more than two variables or a substantial number of cases, you'll certainly want to use a computer. But what computer package should you use?

Regardless of the computer you're using, there are many software packages for doing statistical analysis. Some are intended just for the basics. Others are designed to be full-featured packages that include a vast array of statistical techniques. Even the basic statistical packages typically include a multiple regression procedure, although there are a few exceptions.

All multiple regression packages will give you the statistics found in the tables in Chapter 2: coefficients, standard errors, *t* statistics, and R^2. Any reputable package will also give you the right numerical answers. Many go way beyond that, however, to include such things as diagnostics, graphical displays, automated variable selection, and additional test statistics. Some of these things are very useful; others are merely window dressing. I'll try to give you a general overview of these features and options, but there's no way I can cover them all or discuss them in any detail.

My advice for your initial forays into multiple regression is to choose a package you're familiar with or one that's readily available. If you've already had some experience with a particular statistical package on your computer, by all means use that. Keep in mind that many spreadsheet programs (e.g., Microsoft Excel) have multiple regression functions that produce all the basic output. If you've never used a statistical package before and there's more than one package installed on your computer, find out which one has the reputation for being most easily used. Alternatively, use the package for which you can most easily get help from a friend or coworker.

The decision gets harder when you have a computer with no software that will run a multiple regression. Again, my advice is to start simple. You can easily spend $800 to get a full-featured statistical package, but that's hardly necessary at this point. There are decent regression packages on the market for under $100, and student editions of major statistical packages are often available at very low prices. Get some experience with regression before you make a major investment.

One obvious dividing line among statistical packages—regardless of how extensive or sophisticated—is whether they use a graphical user interface (GUI) or a text interface. With a GUI, you point, click, and drag with a mouse. With a text interface, you type in commands. As a dedicated user of Macintosh computers since they first appeared in 1984, I naturally gravitate to GUIs, yet the statistical package that I use most regularly is the SAS® System, which primarily has a text interface. Packages with GUIs are probably easier for the novice to learn and use, but for complex operations, a text interface is often more straightforward and less cumbersome. In short, it's not a big deal one way or the other. In this chapter, I will be primarily displaying examples that use SPSS®, a comprehensive statistical package that is widely used by researchers and students in the social sciences. SPSS is largely a GUI-based system but also can use text commands for complicated procedures.

4.2. How Do I Get My Data Into the Computer Package?

OK, you have a computer, you have a statistical package running on the computer, and you have some data you want to analyze. What do you do with your data? That depends mainly on what form your data are in now. If the data exist only in hard copy (numbers written or printed on paper), then you'll have to do some typing or hire someone else to do it. Many statistical programs have data entry procedures that make this as painless as possible. The screen display usually consists of something like a spreadsheet with clearly delineated rows and columns that intersect in "cells." Each column corresponds to a particular variable, and each row corresponds to a particular observation (unit of analysis). You simply tab from cell to cell and type in the appropriate number. Incidentally, for nominal variables like religious preference or marital status, it's usually a good idea to create a set of number codes for each of the categories. Some programs will accept alphabetic characters for some statistical operations, but other operations may require numbers.

Figure 4.1 shows the data editor window for SPSS. To set up this screen, I opened SPSS, clicked on the column heading boxes, and then typed in the variable names. For the data in Table 1.1, I have already entered the numbers for the first four observations, and income for the fifth observation. I have also typed the number 14 in the box to the right of **5:school**. If I hit the tab key at this point, the 14 would be entered into the currently highlighted cell, and the highlight box would jump one cell to the right. I can continue typing in numbers like this until all the data are entered.

If your statistical package does not have a data entry procedure, the best way to proceed is to enter the data into a spreadsheet program, which is likely to be very similar to the SPSS data editor. Your statistical package may then be able to directly read the standard file saved by the spreadsheet program. If it doesn't, you can certainly save the spreadsheet file as a text file. This is just a standard computer ASCII file with no labeling information. Virtually all statistical packages can read text files, so this is as close as you'll get to a universal data format.

A text file can also be created by almost any word processing program or text editor, though this is more dangerous than doing it in a spreadsheet because it's easier to put the wrong numbers in the wrong places. Each line of the file should correspond to a single observation or case. There are two different ways to arrange the

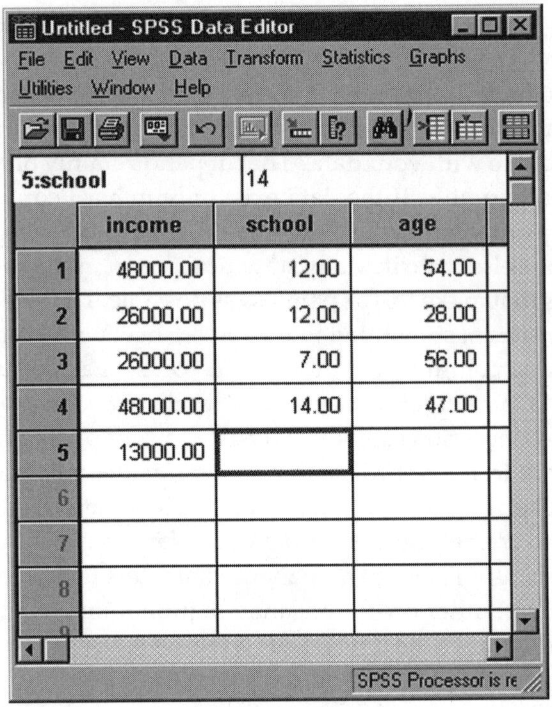

Figure 4.1

variables on each line. With *free format*, you simply type the variable values in order, with at least one space between values. For the income data described in Chapter 1, the first 10 lines of a free-format text file might look like Box 4.1.

BOX 4.1.

```
48000  12  54
26000  12  28
26000  7  56
48000  14  47
13000  14  23
34000  12  60
18000  11  36
24000  16  34
81000  16  61
21000  12  38
9000  6  53
```

With *formatted* input, on the other hand, each variable is assigned to certain numbered columns, and the values must appear in those columns. Although it is not required that you put spaces between the variables in formatted input, the data will be much easier to read (both visually and by the computer) if there are spaces. Formatted input can be annoying, but for data sets with many variables, it's the only way to keep careful track of which variables go where. Box 4.2 shows what the same data might look like in a text file with formatted input.

BOX 4.2.

```
48000 12 54
26000 12 28
26000  7 56
48000 14 47
13000 14 23
34000 12 60
18000 11 36
24000 16 34
81000 16 61
21000 12 38
 9000  6 53
```

Notice how the numbers are nicely aligned in columns. Because this file has spaces between the variable values, it could be read by the statistical package in exactly the same way as the free-format file. If there were no spaces, you would have to tell the package which columns contain which variables.

To read a free-format file, you simply tell the statistical program the name of the text file and then give a list of names for the variables. In SPSS, for example, the dialog box for reading free-format data looks like Figure 4.2.

I typed the names of the variables into the "Name:" box; it's essential that the order of these names be the same as the order in which the variables appear on each line of data.

All statistical packages require that the variables be named. There are usually restrictions on the form these names can take, but some packages are more restrictive than others. Variable names in SPSS, for example, can have no more than eight characters, the first character must be a letter, and there can be no spaces within the name.

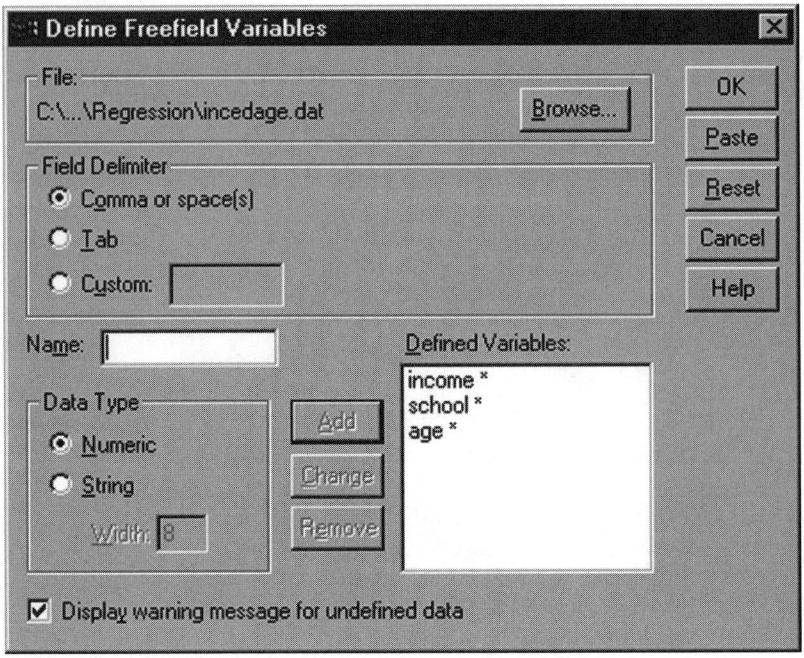

Figure 4.2

If you want to read data from a text file in *fixed* format, in addition to the name of the file and the variables, you must tell the program where to look for the variable values on each data line. Specifically, you must specify the starting and ending column for each variable. The dialog box for reading fixed-format data into SPSS is shown in Figure 4.3. I have already entered the specification for income and school, and I have begun to enter the column specifications for age.

Now let's suppose your data are already in some kind of file that is stored on your own computer, or is accessible over some network. If it's a text file, then we've just seen how to read these files into your statistical package. What other possibilities are there? Like word processing programs, most statistical programs have their own proprietary format for data files. In addition to the numbers that you find in a text file, these files typically include variable names and other information about the variables. The main advantage of proprietary files is that you don't have to specify variable names or variable locations every time you access the data. The package may

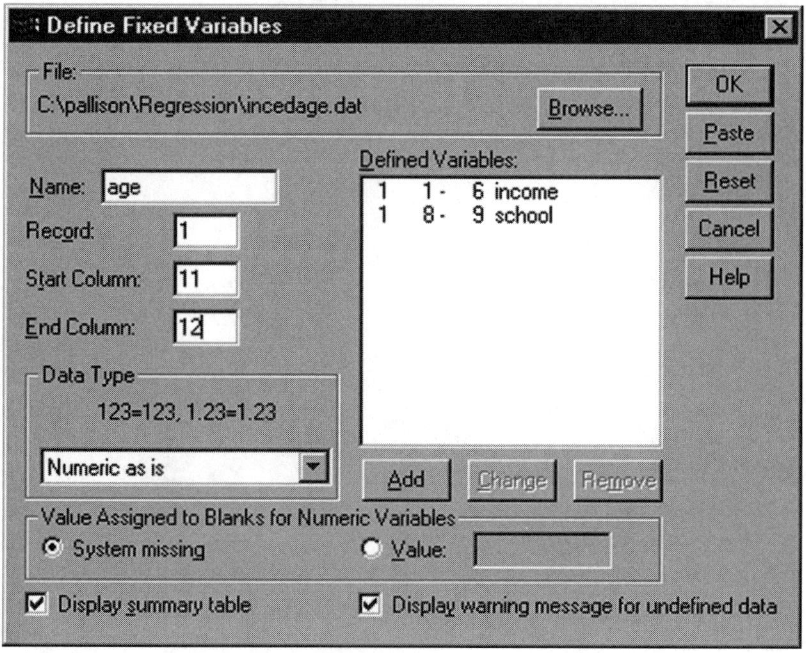

Figure 4.3

also be able to read them more quickly, an important issue for very large data sets. Once you've read the data in from a text file, you can usually save it as a proprietary file.

If the data are currently in the proprietary format for the statistical package you're using, then you're in business. All you need to do is tell your package the name of the file, and you can immediately begin to specify regression models. But what if the data are in a proprietary file from some other statistical package, or from a spreadsheet program? Some statistical programs are able to read data files produced by certain other statistical programs or spreadsheet programs. If so, you're in luck. More likely, however, you'll have to do some conversion. There are programs available that do nothing else but convert data from one proprietary file type to another but, again, these programs can't cover all the possibilities. The only universal solution is to have the original statistical program convert the file into a text file. Then read the text file with the package that you want to use for the analysis.

School

		Frequency	Percent	Valid Percent	Cumulative Percent
Valid	6.00	1	2.9	2.9	2.9
	7.00	3	8.6	8.6	11.4
	8.00	1	2.9	2.9	14.3
	9.00	2	5.7	5.7	20.0
	10.00	1	2.9	2.9	22.9
	11.00	1	2.9	2.9	25.7
	12.00	10	28.6	28.6	54.3
	13.00	1	2.9	2.9	57.1
	14.00	7	20.0	20.0	77.1
	16.00	4	11.4	11.4	88.6
	17.00	1	2.9	2.9	91.4
	18.00	1	2.9	2.9	94.3
	20.00	2	5.7	5.7	100.0
	Total	35	100.0	100.0	

Figure 4.4

4.3. What Else Should I Do Before Running the Multiple Regression?

Once the data have been read by your statistical package, you could immediately begin running regression models. However tempting that may be, it is usually not a good idea. Instead, you should spend some time "cleaning" and checking your data. The first thing to do is request "univariate" statistics for all the variables you intend to work with. The statistics should include things like the mean, the standard deviation, and especially the minimum and maximum values. These statistics will quickly let you know whether you've read the variables properly and whether any variables have very extreme or unusual values. For variables that have a relatively small number of possible values (say, less than 20), you should also request a "one-way" frequency count of each value. Again, the goal is to check for possible errors or unusual values, and to get an idea of how the cases are distributed across the various outcomes. Figure 4.4 shows a one-way frequency count for number of years of schooling, produced by SPSS.

It's easily seen that the maximum (20) and minimum (6) fall within the usual range of years of schooling, and that the frequencies are highest at common ending points for schooling: 12 (high school), 14 (associate degree), and 16 (bachelor's degree). This is all reassuring information about this variable.

Another important issue is missing data. In most data sets, there are some individuals with missing information on some variables. This can happen for many reasons. Maybe the interviewee refused to respond to a particular question, or perhaps the interviewer forgot to ask the question. Regardless of the reason, if you have missing data you must

- Choose some value to represent the missing data,
- Tell the package what value(s) you've chosen, and
- Decide how missing data are to be treated in the regression analysis.

Many statistical packages have a standard code for missing values. In SAS and SPSS, it's a period. In BMDP, it's an asterisk. If you're coding the data yourself and you know what package you'll be using, you can make things easy by using the proper missing value code when you type in the data. When you use other people's data, you'll often find that missing data are coded as some unusual value, like 99 or –1. If the missing data have values other than the default missing value code, then you'll either have to

- Tell the package what the missing value code is, or
- Transform the old code to the standard code.

I won't go into details because every package has a different way of accomplishing these operations.

Then there's the issue of what the multiple regression procedure is supposed to do when it encounters missing data. In most packages, the default is something called *listwise deletion* or *complete case analysis*. With this simple method, if an observation has missing data on any of the variables in the regression model, that observation is completely excluded from the analysis. Although listwise deletion has many desirable properties, it can often end up excluding a large fraction of the sample. A common alternative method is *pairwise deletion*, also known as *available case analysis*. Although this method makes use of more of the data, it has so many undesirable features that it can't be recommended for general use. Even worse than pairwise deletion is replacement with means. In this method, the missing values are replaced with the mean value of the variable for those individuals without missing data. There are better, recently developed methods such as *maximum likelihood* and *multiple imputation*, but these are currently unavailable in commercial regression programs. For most folks, then, the best bet is to stick with listwise deletion.

At this point, you may be ready to do a multiple regression run. Often, however, you'll need to do still more manipulation of the data. If some of your variables are measured at the nominal level, you may have to create dummy variables corresponding to the different categories of the variable. For example, suppose you have a variable named MARSTAT with the following codes:

1 = never married

2 = currently married

3 = divorced or separated

4 = widowed

If you want to include marital status as an independent variable and don't want to lose any of the detail, you'll need to create three dummy variables. Some regression packages can create these dummy variables automatically (see Section 4.6). Most require that you define the variables in transformation statements. For example, in the SPSS syntax editor (NOTE: The SPSS syntax editor is not available in SPSS Version 8 for Students), the statements would look like this:

```
RECODE MARSTAT (2=1)(ELSE=0) INTO CURMAR.
RECODE MARSTAT (3=1)(ELSE=0) INTO DIVORCE.
RECODE MARSTAT (4=1)(ELSE=0) INTO WIDOW.
```

Equivalent operations could be accomplished in a series of dialog boxes. Note that no dummy variable was created for the "never married" group. As explained earlier (and in Chapter 8), the number of dummy variables for a nominal variable must always be one less than the number of categories.

Finally, you may want to do other transformations of your variables before you enter them into a multiple regression model. For example, if you know a person's year of birth and the current year, you'll want to subtract year of birth from current year to get the person's age. For some variables, like income, you may want to work with the logarithm of income rather than income itself. To fit

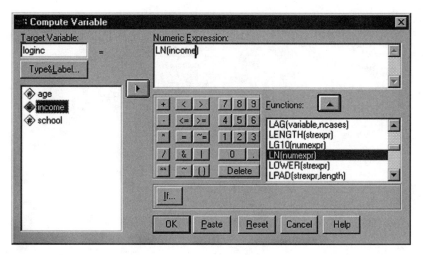

Figure 4.5

nonlinear models, you may have to compute the square or the cube of a variable.

Every program has a somewhat different way of specifying these transformations. For example, Figure 4.5 shows a dialog box that tells SPSS to take the natural logarithm of income to produce a new variable called LOGINC.

4.4. How Do I Indicate Which Regression Model I Want to Run?

Once you have the data ready, you only need to specify two things to run a multiple regression model: the name of the dependent variable and the names of the independent variables. That will usually produce all the information that's presented in the tables in Chapter 2 (with the possible exception of standardized coefficients). For a text-based package, the model is usually specified by writing the names in the form of an equation. Thus, in the SAS system:

```
proc reg;
  model income = school age;
```

The PROC REG statement tells SAS to do a linear regression. The MODEL statement says that the dependent variable is income and the independent variables are school and age.

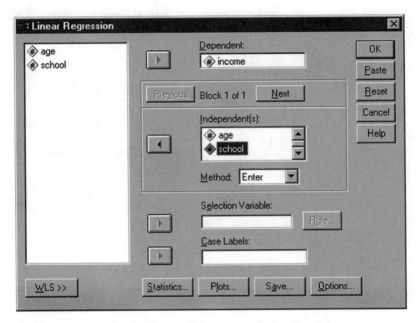

Figure 4.6

For a GUI package, you typically have to click on the name of the dependent variable in one display of variable names and click on the names of the independent variables in another display. Figure 4.6 shows an example from SPSS. In this dialog box, I first clicked on income from the box on the left-hand side. By clicking on the arrow, I moved income into the Dependent box. In a similar fashion, I moved age and school into the Independent box. Clicking on the "OK" button would run the regression.

4.5. How Do I Interpret Computer Output?

Multiple regression packages vary somewhat in terms of what statistics are printed and how they are labeled. In most cases, it's fairly easy to identify the coefficients, standard errors, t statistics, p values, and R^2, but there may also be other statistics that we haven't yet discussed. Let's look at a couple of examples. Figures 4.7, 4.8, and 4.9 display output produced by the SPSS dialog box in Section 4.4.

Model	R	R Square	Adjusted R Square	Std. Error of the Estimate
1	.526[a]	.277	.232	17106.9208

a. Predictors: (Constant), SCHOOL, AGE

Figure 4.7. Model Summary

Model		Sum of Squares	df	Mean Square	F	Sig.
1	Regression	3.58E+09	2	1.79E+09	6.122	.006[a]
	Residual	9.36E+09	32	2.93E+08		
	Total	1.29E+10	34			

a. Predictors: (Constant), SCHOOL, AGE
b. Dependent Variable: INCOME

Figure 4.8. ANOVA[b]

Model		Unstandardized Coefficients		Standardized Coefficients		
		B	Std. Error	Beta	t	Sig.
1	Constant)	−25965.0	15151.061		−1.714	.096
	AGE	600.193	209.893	.435	2.860	.007
	SCHOOL	2056.965	848.834	.369	2.423	.021

a. Dependent Variable: INCOME

Figure 4.9. Coefficients[a]

The "Model Summary" table gives the R^2 and associated statistics. The statistic labeled R is just the square root of R^2. The "adjusted R square" is a modification of the R^2 that adjusts for the number of independent variables. The adjusted R^2 is always less than or equal to the original R^2, and the discrepancy gets larger as the number of independent variables increases. The "standard error of the estimate" (explained at the end of Section 2.5) is a statistic that is primarily useful when constructing confidence intervals around the predicted values from a regression analysis. It usually can be ignored.

Figure 4.8 is titled ANOVA, which stands for *analysis of variance*. In most instances, the only statistic worth looking at in such a table is the one labeled "Sig." for significance level. This is the p value for a test of the null hypothesis that all the coefficients are 0, that is, that the independent variables add nothing to our knowledge of the dependent variable. If the p value is small, as it is in this case, then you can legitimately conclude that *at least one* of the coefficients is *not* 0. Many statisticians argue that if this overall test is not statistically significant, there's no point in looking at the individual coefficients and their p values.

In case you're interested, the p value is based on the F statistic in the preceding column, and that, in turn, is the ratio of the two numbers in the "mean square" column. Each of the mean squares is calculated by dividing the "sum of squares" by its associated *df* (degrees of freedom). The "sum of squares" statistics are described in Section 1.11. The table labeled "Coefficients" presents all the standard regression statistics that should now be familiar from Chapters 1 and 2. The specific numbers reported here were previously discussed in Sections 1.10-1.12. Again, the column labeled "Sig." is the p value for the associated t statistic in the preceding column. Although a p value is reported for the constant (intercept), this will rarely be of any interest.

For comparison, Figure 4.10 shows the corresponding output from the SAS system, produced by the statements in Section 4.4. Most of these statistics are the same as those given by SPSS, although reported with more decimal places.

A few differences from SPSS are worth noting. First, SAS doesn't report standardized coefficients unless you ask for them. Second, the "Root MSE" statistic is the same as the standard error of the estimate. Below that, "Dep Mean" is the mean value of the dependent variable. "C.V.," which stands for coefficient of variation, is calculated by the formula

$$100 \times \text{Root MSE}/\text{Dep Mean}.$$

I don't think I've ever seen anyone report or interpret this statistic.

4.6. What Are the Common Options in Regression Packages?

Besides the statistics displayed above, any good regression package will have numerous optional statistics that you can request, either by typing in the appropriate keyword or by clicking on an option box. Few of these optional statistics ever appear in published

```
Model: MODEL1
  Dependent Variable: INCOME
                  Analysis of Variance
                      Sum of        Mean
  Source    DF     Squares        Square      F Value Prob>F
  Model      2  3582904306.3  1791452153.2    6.122  0.0056
  Error     32  9364695693.7  292646740.43
  C Total   34 12947600000
     Root MSE    17106.92083    R-square    0.2767
     Dep Mean    25200.00000    Adj R-sq    0.2315
     C.V.           67.88461


                  Parameter Estimates


                                          T for H0:
                  Parameter   Standard    Parameter   Prob>
  Variable DF     Estimate      Error       = 0        |T|
  INTERCEP 1       -25965   15151.060863   -1.714     0.0962
  AGE      1  600.192796   209.89336042     2.860     0.0074
  SCHOOL   1 2056.965342   848.83436278     2.423     0.0212
```

Figure 4.10

reports, but some of them can be very useful in identifying problems with the regression analysis or in helping you decide which independent variables should go in the model. What follows is a brief list of the options that are most commonly used or that I think are particularly useful. Some of these will be described in more detail in later chapters.

Standardized Coefficients

Recall that standardized coefficients convert all the variables into standard deviation units. They tell you how many standard deviations the dependent variable changes for an increase of one standard deviation in a particular independent variable. Because all standardized coefficients are in the same metric, you can compare them across different variables. Some regression packages (like SPSS) print these coefficients automatically, but they're optional in

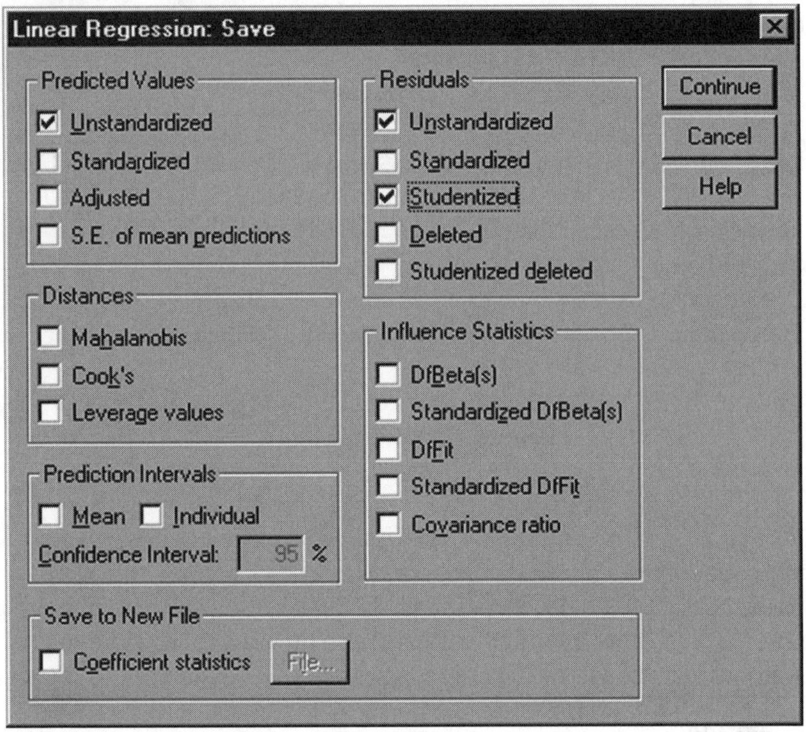

Figure 4.11

most packages. Some people prefer partial correlation coefficients, another option in some packages.

Predicted Values and Residuals

Most packages allow you to print out the predicted values of the dependent variable for all observations, based on the estimated regression equation. This option is often combined with a request for *residuals*, which is another name for prediction errors. These, of course, are just the observed values of the dependent variable minus the predicted values. Many packages will optionally write the predicted values and residuals to another computer file so that you can do additional analysis on them.

The predicted values are obviously useful if you want to make predictions. The residuals are useful in identifying *outliers*, or observations that deviate sharply from the predictions. To make this easier, some programs will also produce *studentized* residuals, which divide each residual by its standard error. Studentized residuals greater than 2.5 (or less than –2.5) are worth looking at closely.

To get predicted values and residuals with SPSS, you click on the "Save" button in the regression dialog box (shown at the end of Section 4.4). This calls up the dialog box shown in Figure 4.11.

Then you simply click on the statistics you want. In this dialog box, I've requested the unstandardized predicted values, the unstandardized residuals, and the studentized residuals. These statistics are added to the original data file. Table 4.1 shows the values for the income data set.

Looking at the last column, we see that only one observation (number 15) has a large studentized residual (3.24814). This observation had a predicted income of $26,327 but an observed income of $81,000.

Confidence Intervals

If you want confidence intervals around your regression coefficients, you can always calculate them yourself using the reported standard errors. For samples of moderate to large size, you can get a 95% confidence interval by adding and subtracting twice the standard error of the reported regression coefficient. Some packages will save you the trouble and print confidence intervals as optional statistics. The default is usually 95% confidence, but you can usually request different confidence levels.

No Intercept

Many packages allow you to fit a regression model in which the intercept term is forced to be equal to zero. This option is rarely needed. Unless you have some very good reason for choosing this option, don't do it.

Automated Coding of Nominal Variables

In Section 4.3, I described how to create a set of dummy variables corresponding to a single nominal variable. On request, some re-

TABLE 4.1

Income	Predicted	Residual	Studentized Residual
48000.00	31129.00996	16870.99004	1.01220
26000.00	15523.99726	10476.00274	.63163
26000.00	22044.56884	3955.43116	.24702
48000.00	31041.59107	16958.40893	1.01081
13000.00	16636.96396	-3636.96396	-.22182
34000.00	34730.16674	-730.16674	-.04444
18000.00	18268.57428	-268.57428	-.01604
24000.00	27353.01540	-3353.01540	-.20216
81000.00	43558.22090	37441.77910	2.33706
21000.00	21525.92522	-525.92522	-.03125
9000.00	18187.02511	-9187.02511	-.58041
18000.00	19125.15403	-1125.15403	-.06712
34000.00	35586.74649	-1586.74649	-.09615
21000.00	25639.85590	-4639.85590	-.27597
81000.00	26327.46759	54672.53241	3.24814
48000.00	47584.73270	415.26730	.02713
6000.00	34048.42477	-28048.4248	-1.89189
21000.00	23839.27751	-2839.27751	-.16923
21000.00	19125.15403	1874.84597	.11184
9000.00	16636.96396	-7636.96396	-.46577
34000.00	29241.01268	4758.98732	.28306
7000.00	11153.67962	-4153.67962	-.25408
24000.00	24101.53419	-101.53419	-.00626
34000.00	29153.59379	4846.40621	.29161
34000.00	33011.13752	988.86248	.06005
4000.00	10722.45489	-6722.45489	-.41510
5000.00	31560.23469	-26560.2347	-1.66225
13000.00	34642.74785	-21642.7478	-1.30110
7000.00	34980.68397	-27980.6840	-1.78477
13000.00	17324.57564	-4324.57564	-.25917
34000.00	6439.55614	27560.44386	1.73854
10000.00	28553.40099	-18553.4010	-1.11693
48000.00	43470.80201	4529.19799	.28426
6000.00	10122.26209	-4122.26209	-.25552
2000.00	9609.48818	-7609.48818	-.46808

gression packages will do this recoding automatically, a huge convenience that can save you a great deal of time and trouble.

Multicollinearity Diagnostics

In Chapter 3 I discussed the problems that can arise when the independent variables are too highly correlated with one another. A common way to judge the seriousness of the multicollinearity problem is to examine all the bivariate correlations among the independent variables. Although this can provide some useful information, it's not sufficient. Because multicollinearity can involve more than two variables at a time, you really need to look at other statistics. Some regression packages can optionally print one or more statistics that are very effective in diagnosing multicollinearity. The ones I find most useful are the *tolerance* statistics, which are calculated for each independent variable. Tolerance values range between 0 and 1. Paradoxically, high tolerance values indicate low multicollinearity, and low tolerance values indicate high multicollinearity. Although there is no strict cutoff, I start to get concerned when the tolerance falls below .40. See Chapter 7 for more details.

Influence Statistics

Residuals and studentized residuals have long been used to identify outliers. In recent years, the identification of unusual observations has focused more heavily on *influence statistics*. These statistics tell you how much the regression results would change if each individual observation were deleted from the analysis. If the deletion of an observation produces a big change, the observation is said to be influential. The influence of an observation depends in part on the size of its residual but also on how extreme its independent variables are. In predicting income from age and schooling, people with very high or very low values on age and schooling will tend to be more influential.

Influence statistics come in both standardized and unstandardized versions. Both can be helpful. The unstandardized statistics tell you how much the actual coefficient would change if that case were deleted. The standardized influence statistics divide the unstandardized statistics by the standard error of the coefficient. This makes it possible to compare the values across different variables.

TABLE 4.2

DFFIT	DFBETA(age)	DFBETA(school)
901.16332	31.60187	−10.12337
668.76647	−23.80398	−32.85575
559.07628	7.32186	−57.32098
673.48608	15.99817	65.48810
−322.09298	10.71175	−6.01252
−61.31100	−2.12228	.01642
−11.88068	.28692	1.31206
−214.00562	3.09163	−26.57114
5248.15050	136.51686	423.44388
−17.57883	.34267	1.10510
−1543.83572	−11.57592	165.61561
−46.63243	1.44440	2.81136
−118.32359	−4.21461	−3.85069
−163.59923	2.14966	−13.88616
1800.96184	32.40692	−73.49777
103.27605	1.30155	9.91819
−9296.20875	**−173.00514**	**405.84176**
−112.45714	2.65404	−7.72301
77.70369	−2.40680	−4.68458
−676.33679	22.49274	−12.62521
168.05064	2.24535	16.94776
−394.54661	8.90863	45.75465
−11.39550	−.19349	1.15583
288.31523	−2.13145	39.65828
78.41549	.13661	11.16380
−778.74467	25.05561	27.60384
−3884.09989	−96.19424	211.57553
−1247.63112	−41.44501	−97.58309
−5334.96654	**21.70012**	**−573.22751**
−220.65620	7.65538	12.15235
4533.94571	−73.56691	−483.83992
−1124.19838	11.13054	−150.18082
691.81522	12.14953	74.15333
−512.86257	16.18008	17.48092
−816.62358	23.34428	68.64489

Table 4.2 shows the unstandardized influence statistics produced by SPSS for the income data. These statistics are added to the original data file, rather than being written to a new file or to the output window.

The column labeled "DFFIT" gives a measure of the overall change in the regression equation that would result from deleting each observation. More specifically, it tells us how much the predicted value for each observation would change if that observation were deleted from the regression analysis. The two columns labeled "DFBETA" tell us how much the coefficient for each of the two independent variables would change if that observation were deleted. Clearly, observation 17 (shown in bold), with a DFFIT of about –9,296, is the most influential observation. The value of income predicted by the age and schooling values (76 and 7, respectively) for this observation would change by more than $9,000 if this observation were deleted from the OLS estimation. Observation 17 also has the most influence on the coefficient for age. Recall that the coefficient for age is $600. If we delete observation 17, the new coefficient would be $173 larger, that is, $773. Observation 17 is also influential for the schooling coefficient, but it is not the most influential. That honor belongs to observation 29 (also shown in bold). The original coefficient for schooling is $2,057. If observation 29 is deleted, the coefficient goes up to $2,630, a change of $573.

As in the case of residuals, influential observations often need special attention. For example, you may want to check each influential observation to make sure that there are no coding errors. This may require that you go back to the original hard copy version of the data, if available, or cross-check the values against other sources of information.

Weighted Regression

Ordinary least squares—the default method for nearly all regression packages—gives the same weight to every observation. Sometimes, however, there are reasons for doing a weighted least squares regression in which some observations are given more weight than others. For example, if your observations are cities, you may want to give more weight to large cities than to small ones. To do a weighted least squares regression, you need an additional variable in the data set which gives the weight to be assigned to each observation. Although weighted least squares can be a useful option, I advise against choosing it unless you have the advice of someone who understands the technical issues involved. For more on this method, see Section 6.6.

There's another kind of weighted regression in which some observations are treated as though they were actually two or more observations. This is quite different from weighted least squares and is useful only in special circumstances. Unfortunately, the documentation for some regression packages is unclear about which kind of weighting is used.

Hypothesis Testing

Standard regression output gives you only two kinds of hypothesis tests: an F test that *all* the coefficients are 0, and t tests for the hypotheses that each coefficient is equal to 0. Sometimes that's not enough. Often you'll want to test whether a set of coefficients are all equal to 0. The most common reason for doing this is when you have a set of dummy variables that correspond to a single nominal variable. To test whether the nominal variable has a significant effect, you need to test the null hypothesis that all the dummy variables have coefficients of 0. Occasionally you may need to test whether two coefficients are equal to each other. Some regression packages have special hypothesis-testing options that make it easy to test hypotheses like these. This facility can be very useful when you need it.

Plots

Many regression packages can produce a wide array of graphical displays that help you visualize the regression equation and diagnose problems. I'll postpone discussing these because we have not yet discussed the geometry of least squares regression. I will say, however, that the plots I find most useful are the partial regression plots and partial residual plots.

Automated Variable Selection

One of the most perplexing parts of doing multiple regression analysis is deciding which variables should be independent variables in the model. In Chapter 3, I argued that certain variables should definitely be in the regression model and that certain variables should definitely not be in the model. There will often be many variables that don't fall clearly within either of these two categories.

Especially common are situations where you have a large pool of potential independent variables—far too many to put all of them in—but no good reasons for choosing some and not others.

It's no surprise, then, that methods of automated variable selection are very popular in regression packages. There are many different methods. The ones that are best known are forward inclusion, backward deletion, stepwise, and best subset. The general goal is the same: to get a parsimonious model that includes those variables with important effects on the dependent variable but excludes those variables that have trivial effects. This is not a straightforward task because the magnitude of a variable's coefficient depends on what other variables are already in the regression model.

Many statisticians take a dim view of automated variable selection methods. The main complaint is that these methods capitalize on chance. If you have a large pool of variables to draw on, you'll almost surely come up with some statistically significant results even if there's nothing going on at all. Because I'm sympathetic to this view, I've never developed much expertise in the relative merits of the various methods, especially the newer ones. On those rare occasions when I use automated methods, I prefer backward deletion.

Chapter Highlights

1. Although bivariate regression can be done easily on a hand calculator, if you have more than two variables or a substantial number of cases, you'll want to use a computer.

2. Nearly all statistical packages and many spreadsheet programs will do multiple regression and provide correct answers and the basic output. The more comprehensive statistical packages have many additional features and options.

3. To put hard-copy data into machine-readable form, use a spreadsheet program or a data entry editor in a statistical package. Rows should correspond to cases, and columns should correspond to variables.

4. Most statistical packages have proprietary file formats for storing data, but all statistical packages can read and write the data as a text file. The easiest text file to read and write is a free format file, with each line corresponding to an observation and variables

separated by spaces. Fixed-format files require that variable values be entered in specified columns.

5. Before running a multiple regression, you should spend some time checking and cleaning the data. This means you should get familiar with the possible values of each variable and, as far as possible, make sure there are no errors in the data.

6. Most data sets have missing data—cases with no information on some of the variables. You must tell your multiple regression package what special codes are used to indicate missing data in your data set.

7. The default method for handling missing data in most packages is listwise deletion—deleting any case that has missing data on any variable in the regression model. Although superior methods (maximum likelihood or multiple imputation) are available in special software, listwise deletion will have to do for the typical user.

8. Before running the regression, you may want to create dummy variables corresponding to nominal variables in the data set. You may also want to transform the variables in ways discussed in Chapter 8.

9. Once the data are in the desired form, requesting the computer to do a multiple regression involves little more than specifying the dependent variable and a list of independent variables.

10. Studentized residuals are useful for finding observations with large discrepancies between the observed and predicted values.

11. Even more useful than residuals are influence statistics. These tell you how much the regression results would change if a particular observation were deleted from the sample. You should examine the data carefully for cases with large influence statistics to make sure there are no errors.

12. Automated variable selection is usually not advisable unless you have a large number of potential independent variables and little prior knowledge that would enable you to make a more principled choice.

Project

Here's a project to help you get experience in doing multiple regression on a computer. On the World Wide Web (http://lib.stat.

cmu.edu/datasets/colleges/) you can download a data set containing information on 1,302 American colleges and universities, originally reported in *U.S. News and World Report's* 1995 *Guide to America's Best Colleges*. There are two versions of the data set: usnews.data contains data in free format, and usnews3.data contains data in fixed format. The free-format data set is "comma delimited," which means that there are commas between each pair of data values rather than spaces. To read this, you may need to give special instructions to your statistical package program. For example, in SPSS, after specifying "Read ASCII data" and "Freefield" from the File menu, you will need to click "Custom" and then enter a comma in the box. Of course, you will have to choose a name for each of the approximately 35 variables. The file usnews.doc contains brief descriptions of each variable and the column numbers for the fixed-format version of the data set. In both versions of the data set, missing data are represented by asterisks. Again, special instructions may be necessary to tell the package that asterisks represent missing data. When SPSS tries to read these data, it rejects an asterisk as a valid value and automatically sets the value as "system missing," which is exactly what you want it to do.

Before doing any regression analyses, you should spend some time getting familiar with the data. Request descriptive statistics on all the variables and examine the means, standard deviations, and maximums and minimums. Pay particular attention to the number of valid (nonmissing) cases. Histograms (bar charts of the frequency distribution) can give you a good idea of how the data are distributed across different possible values of the variables.

Your goal should be to develop and estimate a multiple regression model in which the dependent variable is the *graduation rate*. This is the percentage of undergraduate students who graduate, out of those who enroll. The choice of independent variables is up to you, but there are a couple of points worth keeping in mind. First, if you include variables with a lot of missing data, you could end up with a very small number of cases actually used in the analysis, so it may be desirable to stick with variables that have at least 1,000 cases. Second, be careful about including variables that are highly correlated with each other and are just minor variants of the same thing (for example, percentage of faculty with Ph.D.s and percentage of faculty with terminal degrees). Chapter 8 discusses the problems with such variables. Multicollinearity diagnostics can help you avoid these problems.

You may also want to transform some of the variables. For example, instead of including "number of applications received" and "number of applicants accepted" in the model, you may want to convert to a variable stating number of applicants accepted divided by number of applications received. Try removing variables from the model that are not statistically significant, and see how this changes the results.

5 How Does Bivariate Regression Work?

If you've made it this far in the book, you already know much of what you need to be an intelligent user of multiple regression. If no one is making you read this book, you may decide that you don't want to go any further. Nevertheless, it's hard to learn too much about multiple regression: Regression is such a widely used technique that virtually any additional knowledge or understanding is bound to pay off at some point.

With that in mind, we begin a series of chapters that delve a little more deeply into the algebra, geometry, mechanics, and philosophy of least squares regression. This chapter deals with the simplest setting of a dependent variable y and a single independent variable x. That may seem a little too simple because the main attractiveness of regression lies in its ability to control for other variables. Unfortunately, both the algebra and geometry become much more complicated in the three-variable case, so it's essential to begin a step lower. Even in bivariate regression, we'll have to introduce some mathematical notation.

5.1. How Do We Picture the Least Squares Regression Problem?

To understand bivariate regression, it's helpful to have a picture of the data. Figure 5.1 shows a scatterplot of income by age for the data in Table 1.1. Each little square on this graph represents one of the 35 observations in the data set. For example, the square nearest the lower right-hand corner corresponds to a person 76 years old who had an annual income of $6,000. Although there appears to be

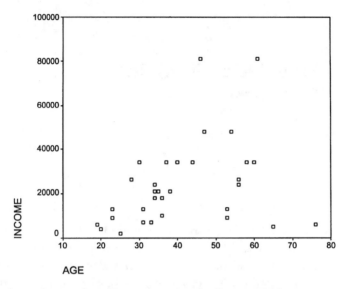

Figure 5.1. Scatterplot of Income on Age for Data in Table 1.1

a general trend of income increasing with age, the relationship is far from perfect.

If we think that the relationship between age and income is best described by a straight line, our problem is to find a line that comes close to the points on the graph. We could, of course, put a ruler on the graph and draw a line that looks like it comes close to many of the points, but someone else could come along and draw a quite different line. How can we tell whose line is better?

In Chapter 1, we introduced the least squares criterion: Choose a line that minimizes the sum of squared prediction errors. Figure 5.2 shows the same scatterplot, but with the least squares regression line added. As you can see, the line passes directly through some of the points but is quite distant from some of the others.

Where did the line come from? Well, I simply asked my graphics program to add a least squares regression line. The program produced the line by performing some simple calculations that we'll discuss in a moment. Those calculations minimize the sum of squared prediction errors (also called residuals). Figure 5.3 shows the prediction errors for this regression line. The errors are represented by vertical lines from each data point to the regression line. The length of each line corresponds to the size of the error. Errors above the regression line are positive; errors below the line are negative.

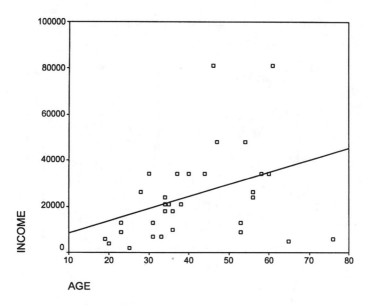

Figure 5.2. Scatterplot With Least Squares Regression Line

Before discussing how the least squares line is calculated, a few things should be noted about this graph.

- As explained in Chapter 1, the regression line corresponds to the general equation $y = a + bx$,

where a and b are numbers to be calculated. Choosing a line is equivalent to choosing a and b.

- The value of a corresponds to the point on the vertical axis where it is crossed by the regression line. We see from the graph that it's around $3,000.
- The slope of the line corresponds to b. In this case, it tells us how much income increases for each 1-year increase in age.
- Although it may not be readily apparent, the line passes through the point $(\bar{x}, \bar{y})$, the intersection of the mean of y and the mean of x. For any bivariate regression, the least squares line will pass through the two means.

5.2. How Is the Least Squares Regression Line Calculated?

To get a regression line, we must find values for a and b in the linear equation $y = a + bx$. The least squares method says to choose

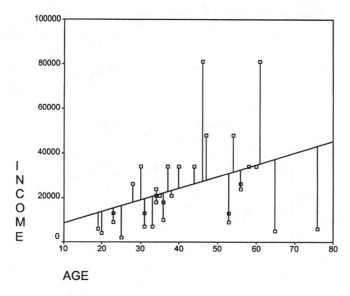

Figure 5.3. Scatterplot With Regression Line and Error Lines

values that minimize the sum of squared residuals. To see how this is accomplished, we need some algebraic notation. Suppose we label each individual in the sample by a number, starting at 1 and going up to n (the number of cases in the sample). The order of the numbers doesn't matter, just so each individual has a unique number. Let i be a variable corresponding to the number. For individual i, let y_i be that individual's value of y and let x_i be that individual's value of x. Thus, x_1 is the value of x for individual 1.

If a and b are possible values of the intercept and slope, the predicted value of y for individual i is just $a + bx_i$. For each individual in the sample, the residual is the observed value of y minus the predicted value of y. The residual, then, is $y_i - (a + bx_i)$. We can therefore represent the sum of *squared* residuals as

$$\sum_i [y_i - (a + bx_i)]^2$$

The capital Greek sigma (Σ) is a common symbol, used to represent summation. The i underneath it means to sum over all the possible values of i, that is, all the individuals in the sample.

As noted in Chapter 1, we could simply try out different values of a and b until we found the ones that produced the smallest sum of squared residuals. That would be a rather inefficient and time-consuming process, however. Instead, differential calculus can be used to derive formulas for the values of a and b that minimize the sum of squared residuals. These formulas can be used in any sample. The formula for the slope b is

$$b = \frac{\sum_i (y_i - \bar{y})(x_i - \bar{x})}{\sum_i (x_i - \bar{x})^2}$$

In words, this formula says to take each value of y and subtract the mean of y. This is sometimes called a *deviation score*. Similarly, take each value of x and subtract the mean of x. To get the numerator in the formula for b, we multiply the two deviation scores for each individual, then add them up for all individuals. To get the denominator, we square the deviation score for x for each individual, then add them all together.

The denominator in this formula may look familiar. The formula for the sample variance of x is

$$s^2 = \frac{\sum_i (x_i - \bar{x})^2}{n - 1}$$

It follows that if we divide the denominator in the formula for b by $n - 1$, we get the sample variance of x. If we divide the numerator in the formula for b by $n - 1$, we get something called the covariance of x and y:

$$s_{xy} = \frac{\sum_i (y_i - \bar{y})(x_i - \bar{x})}{n - 1}$$

The covariance is a statistic that is not often interpreted itself, but is typically used as an intermediate step in getting other statistics. Note that the covariance of a variable with itself is just the variance of that variable, that is, $s_{xx} = s_x^2$.

We can put these two results together to get a more compact formula for b. If we divide the covariance of x and y by the variance of x, the $n - 1$ cancels out of the numerator and the denominator, and we're left with our formula for b. We can say, then, that the least squares slope coefficient is equal to the sample covariance of x and y divided by the sample variance of x, or $b = s_{xy}/s_x^2$.

This is the formula for b that I find easiest to remember.

We'll meet the covariance again when we talk about correlation. Right now, we still need a formula for a, the least squares intercept. Earlier, I said that the least squares line must always pass through the point $(\bar{x}, \bar{y})$. That implies that we can write the equation

$$\bar{y} = a + b\bar{x}.$$

If we solve this equation for a, we get

$$a = \bar{y} - b\bar{x},$$

and this becomes our formula for the intercept. This formula tells us to first calculate b, then multiply b by the mean of x, and then subtract the result from the mean of y.

Table 5.1 displays the intermediate calculations necessary for computing a and b for our age and income example. The second and third columns are just the data for income and age. We first get the means for these two variables by dividing the totals by the sample size, 35:

$$\bar{x} = 1{,}462/35 = 41.77$$

$$\bar{y} = 882{,}000/35 = 25{,}200.$$

The next two columns simply subtract these means from the original data to get the deviation scores. Notice that the deviation scores necessarily sum to 0. The sixth column multiplies the x and y deviation scores together, and the last column is the square of the deviation scores for x.

To get b, we simply take the ratio of the totals for the last two columns:

$$b = 3{,}559{,}600/6{,}796.17 = 523.76.$$

This tells us that each additional year of age is associated with a \$524 increase in income. To get a, we calculate

$$a = 25{,}200 - (523.76 \times 41.77) = 3{,}323.$$

Our final regression equation is then

$$y = 3{,}323 + 523.76x.$$

TABLE 5.1 Calculations for Regression of Income on Age

i	Income y_i	Age x_i	$y_i - \bar{y}$	$x_i - \bar{x}$	$(x_i - \bar{x})(y_i - \bar{y})$	$(x_i - \bar{x})^2$
1	48,000	54	22,800	12.23	278,844	149.57
2	26,000	28	800	–13.77	–11,016	189.61
3	26,000	56	800	14.23	113,840	202.49
4	48,000	47	22,800	5.23	119,244	27.35
5	13,000	23	–12,200	–18.77	228,994	352.31
6	34,000	60	8,800	18.23	160,424	332.33
7	18,000	36	–7,200	–5.77	415,440	33.29
8	24,000	34	–1,200	–7.77	93,240	60.37
9	81,000	61	55,800	19.23	1,073,034	369.79
10	21,000	38	–4,200	–3.77	158,340	14.21
11	9,000	53	–16,200	11.23	–181,926	126.11
12	18,000	34	–7,200	–7.77	559,440	60.37
13	34,000	58	8,800	16.23	142,824	263.41
14	21,000	38	–4,200	–3.77	158,340	14.21
15	81,000	46	55,800	4.23	236,034	17.89
16	48,000	54	22,800	12.23	278,844	149.57
17	6,000	76	–19,200	34.23	–657,216	1,171.69
18	21,000	35	–4,200	–6.77	284,340	45.83
19	21,000	34	–4,200	–7.77	326,340	60.37
20	9,000	23	–16,200	–18.77	304,074	352.31
21	34,000	44	8,800	2.23	196,240	4.97
22	7,000	31	–18,200	–10.77	196,014	115.99
23	24,000	56	–1,200	14.23	–17,076	202.49
24	34,000	37	8,800	–4.77	–41,976	22.75
25	34,000	40	8,800	–1.77	–15,576	3.13
26	4,000	20	–21,200	–21.77	461,524	473.93
27	5,000	65	–20,200	23.23	–469,246	539.63
28	13,000	53	–12,200	11.23	–137,006	126.11
29	7,000	33	–18,200	–8.77	159,614	76.91
30	13,000	31	–12,200	–10.77	131,394	115.99
31	34,000	30	8,800	–11.77	–103,576	138.53
32	10,000	36	–15,200	–5.77	877,040	33.29
33	48,000	54	22,800	12.23	278,844	149.57
34	6,000	19	–19,200	–22.77	437,184	518.47
35	2,000	25	–23,200	–16.77	389,064	281.23
Total	882,000	1,462	0	0.0	3,559,600	6,796.17

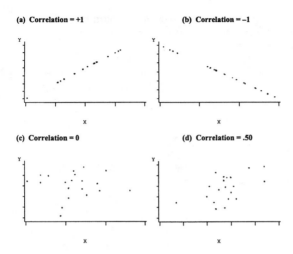

Figure 5.4. Scatterplots for Correlations of Various Sizes

5.3. How Is Regression Related to Correlation?

The regression line is a way of describing the relationship between two variables x and y. Another popular way of describing the relationship between two variables is the correlation coefficient. More precisely, it's called the *Pearson product-moment correlation coefficient*. It turns out that there is a very close relationship between the regression line and the correlation coefficient. In fact, they can be thought of as two alternative ways of describing the same thing. Let's see how.

The correlation coefficient can have any value between -1 and $+1$. If the correlation between x and y is $+1$, then there is a perfect linear relationship between the two variables. That means that if we draw a scatterplot for data on x and y, the points will all lie exactly on a straight line, as in Figure 5.4a. In Figure 5.4b, we see a scatterplot for a correlation of -1. Again there is a perfect linear relationship between x and y, but now it's an *inverse* relationship: As x increases, y decreases.

In Figure 5.4c, we see a scatterplot for two variables that have a correlation of 0. In this case, there is *no* linear relationship between x and y. If we were to draw a least squares regression line for Figure 5.4c, it would be a horizontal line passing through the mean of y. In other words, the slope would be 0.

Finally, Figure 5.4d shows a scatterplot corresponding to a correlation of .50. In this graph, there is a clear tendency for y to go up as x goes up, but if we drew a least squares regression line, there would be a good deal of scatter around the line. This plot looks vaguely similar to the plot for age and income in Figure 5.1. In fact, the correlation for that plot is .38, not very far from .50.

In general, we say that the correlation coefficient measures the *degree of scatter* around a regression line. The slope coefficient b, on the other hand, measures the steepness of the regression line. With one exception, the magnitude of the slope has nothing to do with the degree of scatter. It's possible to have a very steep line with a lot of scatter or a very shallow line with little scatter. The exception is that when the slope is 0 the correlation must also be 0, and vice versa. This fact can be seen by comparing the formulas for the two statistics. As we saw earlier, one simple formula for the slope is $b = s_{xy}/s_x^2$, the covariance of x and y divided by the variance of x. The correlation coefficient, often denoted by the letter r, can be written as

$$r_{xy} = \frac{s_{xy}}{s_x s_y}$$

In words, the correlation is equal to the covariance of x and y divided by the standard deviation of x multiplied by the standard deviation of y. What's important here is that both r and b have the same numerator—the covariance. It follows that if one of them is equal to zero, the other must also be zero. Although that may seem like just a mathematical curiosity, it also has a major practical implication: Testing the hypothesis that $r = 0$ is equivalent to testing whether $b = 0$. There's no need for two distinct tests.

There's another way in which the correlation coefficient is related to regression. In Chapter 1, we discussed the statistic R^2 as a measure of how well we could predict the dependent variable from knowledge of the independent variables. In a bivariate regression, it turns out that the R^2 is equal to the squared correlation between x and y, that is, r^2. In fact, that's how R^2 got its name (or symbol). This can be generalized by the following principle: For any multiple regression, the R^2 is equal to the squared correlation between the observed values of the dependent variable and the predicted values of the dependent variable.

There is one final point to keep in mind about regression and correlation. Because both statistics measure the *linear* relationship

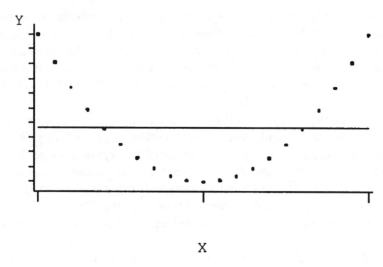

Figure 5.5. A Nonlinear Relationship Between Two Variables

between two variables, they can be highly misleading if the true relationship is very nonlinear. Consider the graph in Figure 5.5. As the scatterplot shows, y can be perfectly predicted from knowledge of x, but the relationship is *quadratic* rather than linear. As x increases, y sometimes decreases and sometimes increases. The net result is that the regression line (the solid, horizontal line) has a slope of 0. Naturally, the correlation coefficient is also zero. If all we knew about the relationship between x and y were the correlation and the slope, we would be seriously mistaken in our assessment of the relationship between these two variables.

5.4. How Is the Standard Error Calculated?

Another important statistic in any regression application is the standard error of the slope coefficient. (The intercept also has a standard error, but we're usually not very interested in that.) We need the standard error of the slope so that we can construct a confidence interval or a test statistic. There are a variety of equivalent formulas for the standard error. I like the one below because it is expressed in terms of statistics we've already encountered and because it is easily interpreted:

$$s.e.\ (b) = \frac{s_y}{s_x}\sqrt{\frac{1 - r^2_{xy}}{n - 2}}$$

In this formula, s_y and s_x are the standard deviations of y and x. The sample size is n, and r^2_{xy} is the squared correlation between x and y (equivalently, the R^2). For the age and income regression, the standard deviation of income is 19,514 and the standard deviation of age is 14.13. The R^2 is .144 and the sample size is 35. Putting them all together, we have

$$\frac{19,514}{14.13}\sqrt{\frac{1 - .144}{35 - 2}} = 222$$

A closer look at the formula for the standard error can tell us some interesting things. First, the fact that n is in the denominator means that the standard error gets smaller as the sample gets larger. Of course, this is true for the standard error of almost any statistic: The bigger the sample, the more precisely we can estimate the statistic. Second, although the squared correlation is in the numerator, it's subtracted from 1. Consequently, as the correlation gets larger in magnitude, the standard error gets smaller. Again, this makes sense. When all the data points are close to the line, we can get very good estimates of the slope, but when there's a large amount of scatter around the line, our estimates of the slope become very imprecise. Finally, note that the standard deviation of x is in the denominator. This means that we get better estimates when there is a lot of variation in the *independent variable*. This can be an important consideration in the design of empirical studies.

Now that we've calculated our standard error of 222, let's see what we can do with it. Recall that the slope coefficient was 524 (rounded). To test the null hypothesis that the true slope is zero, we simply take the ratio of the coefficient to its standard error, 524 / 222 = 2.36. If the sample had more than 100 cases or so, we could simply treat this statistic as a *standard normal variable*. In that case, anything over 2 would be considered statistically significant, and we could conclude that the true slope is *not* zero. Because our sample is only 35 cases, we need to use a t table (found in any introductory statistics textbook). To use a t table, you must know the *degrees of freedom (df)*.

For a bivariate regression, the number of degrees of freedom is $n - 2$ or, in our case, 33. Most t tables give values for 30 df and 40 df, but not for the values in between. We'll use 30 because it's both closer and more conservative. For a two-tailed test, at the .05 level and 30 df, the *critical value* for statistical significance is 2.04. Anything greater than 2.04 or less than –2.04 is said to be statistically significant. So we can say that the coefficient for age is significantly different from zero, which means that there's some evidence that age is related to income.

The other thing we can do with the standard error is construct a confidence interval. To get a 95% confidence interval, we first multiply the standard error by the critical t value for a two-tailed, .05 test. As we just saw, that critical value is 2.04. So $2.04 \times 222 = 453$. Then we both add and subtract this number from the slope coefficient:

$$524 - 453 = 71$$

$$524 + 453 = 977$$

Then, we can say with 95% confidence that the true slope lies somewhere between 71 and 977. That's a pretty wide interval, but, of course, the sample is rather small. The interpretation of the confidence interval is this: If we repeated this procedure many times (with a different sample of 35 cases each time), about 95% of the confidence intervals that we calculated would contain the true value. The accuracy of that statement depends on several assumptions that are discussed in the next chapter.

5.5. How Is Bivariate Regression Related to Trivariate Regression?

As I mentioned at the beginning of this chapter, it's a shame that we have to focus on bivariate regression because regression doesn't really get interesting until we have at least two independent variables. But the mathematics gets rather complicated with multiple independent variables. Nevertheless, when there are just two independent variables, it turns out that the mathematics can be translated into things we've already learned about bivariate regression. This can help us understand in what sense regression allows us to statistically control for variables.

In this chapter we've been looking at the relationship between income and age. Now we'll add the third variable in Table 1.1, years of schooling. Let y be income, x be age, and z be years of schooling. We want to estimate a linear equation of the form

$$y = a + b_1 x + b_2 z.$$

Let's focus on b_1, the effect of x on y, controlling for z. As already noted, many hand calculators have special functions for doing bivariate regression. I'm now going to explain how to use such a calculator to calculate b_1. Before I do so, I want to make it clear that I am not recommending this method for routine use. If you want to do a multiple regression, do it on a computer with an appropriate regression program. The reason for considering this alternative method is to get some insight into how multiple regression works.

We can get b_1 by doing three bivariate regressions. I'll list them first, then explain the details.

1. Regress y on z (that is, take y as the dependent variable and z as the independent variable). Calculate the *residuals* from this regression and call them y^*.

2. Regress x on z. Calculate the *residuals* from this regression and call them x^*.

3. Regress y^* on x^*.

The slope from the third regression will be b_1, exactly the same as if we had used a full-scale multiple regression program.

Now let's look at the details. Step 1 produces the regression equation

$$\hat{y} = 3{,}732 + 1{,}692 z_i.$$

The "hat" over the y means that this is the *predicted* value of y. To get the residuals, we subtract the predicted value of y from the observed value of y for each individual:

$$y_i^* = y_i - \hat{y}_i.$$

These residuals are shown in the "Income Residual" column of Table 5.2.

Step 2 produces the regression equation

$$\hat{x}_i = 49.48 - .608 z_i.$$

TABLE 5.2 Income, Age, and Schooling, With Residuals

Income	Schooling	Age	Age Residual	Income Residual
48,000	12	54	11.8	23,960
26,000	12	28	−14.2	1,960
26,000	7	56	10.8	10,422
48,000	14	47	6.0	20,576
13,000	14	23	−18.0	−14,424
34,000	12	60	17.8	9,960
18,000	11	36	−6.8	−4,347
24,000	16	34	−5.8	−6,809
81,000	16	61	21.2	50,191
21,000	12	38	−4.2	−3,040
9,000	6	53	7.2	−4,886
18,000	12	34	−8.2	−6,040
34,000	13	58	16.4	8,268
21,000	14	38	−3.0	−6,424
81,000	12	46	3.8	56,960
48,000	20	54	16.7	10,422
6,000	7	76	30.8	−9,578
21,000	14	35	−6.0	−6,424
21,000	12	34	−8.2	−3,040
9,000	14	23	−18.0	−18,424
34,000	14	44	3.0	6,576
7,000	9	31	−13.0	−11,963
24,000	8	56	11.4	6,729
34,000	16	37	−2.8	3,191
34,000	17	40	.8	1,499
4,000	12	20	−22.2	−20,040
5,000	9	65	21.0	−13,963
13,000	14	53	12.0	−14,424
7,000	20	33	−4.3	−30,578
13,000	12	31	−11.2	−11,040
34,000	7	30	−15.2	18,422
10,000	16	36	−3.8	−20,809
48,000	18	54	15.5	13,807
6,000	12	19	−23.2	−18,040
2,000	10	25	−18.4	−18,655

The predicted values from this equation are then used to calculate the residuals

$$x_i^* = x_i - \hat{x}_i.$$

These are shown in the "Age Residual" column of Table 5.2.

Why do we want the residuals? Our aim is to estimate the effect of x on y, controlling for z. By calculating residuals, x^* and y^*, we get new versions of x and y that remove or "purge" any relationship with z. Specifically, because independent variables are always uncorrelated with the residuals, the correlation of the age residual with schooling is necessarily 0, and the correlation of the income residual with schooling is also 0. Now we can examine the relationship between x^* and y^* without having to be concerned about any mutual dependence on z.

Step 3 produces the equation

$$\hat{y}_i^* = 600x_i^*$$

which is exactly the slope we got in Chapter 1 using a regular regression program. Notice that there's no intercept in this equation, which is characteristic of this multistep process.

The standard error given by the hand calculator is 207, which is a little smaller than the 210 produced by a multiple regression program. The reason is this. The calculator uses the formula for the standard error that I gave in Section 5.4 but that is appropriate only for a *bivariate* regression. For a trivariate regression, the $n - 2$ in the denominator must be changed to $n - 3$. The hand calculator doesn't know to do this, but we can correct it by multiplying its standard error by $\sqrt{(n-2)/(n-3)}$. When we multiply 207 by $\sqrt{33/32}$ we get exactly the right standard error of 210.

Now we have the slope and standard error for x, controlling for z. If we also want the slope and standard error for z controlling for x, we have to repeat the three steps with z and x interchanged:

1. Regress y on x. Calculate the *residuals* from this regression and call them y^{**}.

2. Regress z on x. Calculate the *residuals* from this regression and call them z^*.

3. Regress y^{**} on z^*.

Again, this gives us exactly the same slope coefficient for z that we would get in a multiple regression program, but it still doesn't give us the intercept in the full trivariate equation. To get that, we must calculate

$$\bar{a} = y - b_1\bar{x} - b_2\bar{z}.$$

As you can see, the process gets a bit tedious, which is why I can't recommend it for routine use. The important thing to remember is that each slope in the trivariate regression can be interpreted as a bivariate slope where the two variables have been purged of their relationship with the third variable. For more details, see McClendon (1994).

One final point is that we can also calculate the correlation between x^* and y^*, the residuals from the bivariate regressions on z. This correlation is called the *partial correlation* and it is often written as $r_{xy.z}$. For our example, the partial correlation between age and income controlling for schooling is .45. The partial correlation between schooling and income controlling for age is .39.

5.6. Why Are There Two Bivariate Regression Lines?

In Section 5.2, we calculated the least squares regression line as

$$y = 3{,}323 + 524x$$

where y is income and x is age. Suppose we turn the problem around and take age as the dependent variable and income as the independent variable. Although that may not make sense from a causal point of view, there's nothing in the mathematics to prevent it. If we then calculate the least squares regression line for predicting x from y, we get

$$x = 34.84 + .000275y.$$

Do these two equations represent the same line? To find out, we can solve the new equation for y. A little algebra produces

$$y = -126{,}691 + 3{,}636x.$$

Clearly the lines are not the same. The second line has a slope that is nearly seven times the size of the slope in the first equation. This is also evident if we graph the two regression lines, as in Figure 5.6. The line with the steeper slope corresponds to the least squares regression with age as the dependent variable and income as the independent variable.

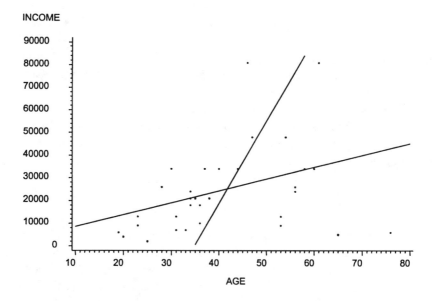

Figure 5.6. Regressions of Income on Age and Age on Income

There's nothing unusual about this. For any two variables x and y, the least squares regression of y on x will produce a different line from the least squares regression of x on y. There's one exception: If the correlation between x and y is 1 or –1, the two regression lines will coincide. The opposite extreme is when the correlation between x and y is 0. Then one regression line will be exactly vertical (at the mean of x), and the other will be exactly horizontal (at the mean of y), forming a cross. Regardless of the correlation, the point where the two lines intersect is always $(\bar{x}, \bar{y})$.

Why are there two different regression lines? Remember that least squares regression is always trying to minimize the sum of squared prediction errors in the dependent variable. The basic fact is that prediction errors in one variable aren't the same as prediction errors in another variable. In Figure 5.6, prediction errors in income would be represented by vertical lines from the data points to the regression line. Prediction errors in age would be represented by *horizontal* lines from the data points to the regression line. Minimizing one kind of prediction error does not produce the same result as minimizing prediction errors in a different variable.

Unfortunately, some people mistakenly believe that the two regression lines can represent reciprocal causation, with x causing y and y causing x. One regression line is supposed to show the effect of x on y, whereas the other line shows the effect of y on x. Although reciprocal causation is often a realistic possibility, the two regression lines do not help us distinguish the two causal directions. One indication of this is that the two slope coefficients must have the same sign. This is easily seen from their formulas. Letting b_{yx} be the slope from regressing y on x, and b_{xy} be the slope from regressing x on y, we have

$$b_{yx} = \frac{s_{xy}}{s_x^2}, \quad b_{xy} = \frac{s_{xy}}{s_y^2}$$

The denominators in both formulas must be greater than 0, so the signs will depend on the numerators, which are the same in both formulas. Why is this important? Well, when we think about reciprocal causation, we usually want to allow for the possibility that the signs may be different. For example, deviant behavior is likely to increase punishment, but punishment may *decrease* deviant behavior. That's not possible if the effects are measured by the two least squares regression lines. If you really want to study reciprocal causation, you must use much more complex methods that also require more elaborate data.

Chapter Highlights

1. In a bivariate regression, the least squares regression line always passes through the intersection of the means of the two variables.

2. The slope of the least squares regression line of y on x is given by s_{xy}/s_x^2. In this formula, the numerator is the covariance of x and y, and the denominator is the variance of x.

3. The intercept of the least squares regression line of y on x is given by $\bar{y} - b\bar{x}$, where b is the least squares slope.

4. The correlation coefficient is calculated as $s_{xy}/(s_x s_y)$, where the numerator is the covariance of x and y and the denominator is the product of their standard deviations.

5. The correlation measures the degree of scatter around a regression line. If it's 1 or −1, all the data points lie on a straight line.

6. The sign of the correlation coefficient is always the same as the sign of the regression slope; therefore, if one is 0, the other is also 0. Testing the hypothesis that the correlation is 0 is always equivalent to testing the hypothesis that the slope is 0.

7. In both bivariate and multiple regression, the R^2 is equal to the squared correlation between the observed values of the dependent variable and the predicted values of the dependent variable.

8. Both the regression slope and the correlation coefficient measure the *linear* relationship between two variables. If the relationship is nonlinear, y could be a perfect function of x, yet the correlation could be small or even 0.

9. The standard error of the regression slope is used to calculate confidence intervals and test statistics. A large standard error means an unreliable estimate of the coefficient.

10. The standard error goes up with the variance in y. The standard error goes down with the sample size, the variance in x, and the R^2.

11. The ratio of the slope coefficient to its standard error is a t statistic, which can be used to test the null hypothesis that the coefficient is 0. With samples larger than 100, a t statistic greater than 2 (or less than –2) means that the coefficient is statistically significant (.05 level, two-tailed test).

12. With samples larger than 100, we can get a confidence interval around a regression coefficient by adding and subtracting twice its standard error.

13. For a trivariate regression of y on x and z, the slope for x can be thought of as arising from a bivariate regression of y^* on x^*, where y^* represents residuals from regressing y on z and x^* represents the residuals from regressing x on z. This helps us understand what it means to "control" for z.

14. The regression of y on x produces a different regression line from the regression of x on y. The two lines cross at the intersection of the two means. The two slopes always have the same sign. The two lines coincide when x and y are perfectly correlated.

Questions to Think About

1. Suppose you have a sample in which the mean income is $32,000 and the mean age is 44. You estimate a bivariate regression of

income on age. Based on the estimated regression model, what's the predicted income for a 44-year-old?

2. For the sample described in question 1, the standard deviation of income is 8,000, the standard deviation of age is 10, and the correlation between age and income is .30. What is the least squares regression line for income on age? (Hint: The correlation can be transformed into the regression slope by appropriate multiplication and division by the standard deviations.)

3. Table 5.3, taken from *USA Today* (December 28, 1984), reports findings by N. Glenn and B. A. Shelton. Regress the divorce rate on the mobility rate. Do it first by hand and then on a computer or calculator. What is the least squares regression line? What is the R^2? Is the coefficient for mobility significantly different from 0? Do you think it's appropriate to interpret the coefficient for mobility as a causal effect on divorce? Why or why not? What important variables might have been left out of this regression? Is reverse causation possible?

TABLE 5.3

Region	Mobility Rate	Divorce Rate
New England	41	4.0
Middle Atlantic	37	3.4
East North Central	44	5.1
West North Central	46	4.6
South Atlantic	47	5.6
East South Central	44	6.0
West South Central	50	6.5
Mountain	57	7.6
Pacific	56	5.9

4. A researcher is studying the relationship between IQ and GPA for a sample of college students. She finds a correlation of .20 among men and .30 among women. Does this mean that the regression lines are different for men and women?

5. Dr. Jones believes that college students who have a lot of friends are more likely to be satisfied with their college experience. Based on a telephone survey at his college, he finds that the correlation between self-reported number of friends and college satisfaction is .35, which is statistically significant at the .01 level.

Dr. Smith says that Jones should also do a linear regression to test his hypothesis. Is Smith right?

6. Using data from the past 2 years, a weather forecaster estimates a multiple regression model in which the dependent variable is the amount of rainfall on a given day and the independent variables include many climatological measurements taken on the previous day. His regression model has an R^2 of .64. Another forecaster claims that he can make "better" predictions by applying a completely different technique known as "neural networks" to the same data. How can the predictions be compared? Can you think of a way to calculate an R^2 for the predictions based on neural networks?

7. For a sample of 1,000 dry cleaning establishments, a marketing researcher finds that the correlation between advertising expenditures and net profit is only .02, which is not statistically significant. Is he justified in concluding that advertising is useless?

8. Suppose an educational researcher wants to estimate a regression model for the relationship between age and hours per day spent on homework. He has a choice between doing the study in a middle school or in a school with kindergarten through 12th grade. On purely statistical grounds, why is he better off with the comprehensive school?

9. Based on a sample of size 250, a regression coefficient of −.753 has a standard error of .310. Is this statistically significant? Calculate a 95% confidence interval for this coefficient.

10. Section 5.5 explained how a trivariate regression could be calculated by running multiple bivariate regressions. Suppose that for the regression of x on z, the R^2 is 1.0. What problem does this create?

6 What Are the Assumptions of Multiple Regression?

Most users of multiple regression are aware that the validity of the technique depends on whether certain assumptions are satisfied, but there is enormous confusion about just what those assumptions are, how they might be violated, and what happens if they are violated. There are several reasons for this confusion. One is that there is no single set of assumptions on which everyone agrees. Rather, there are a number of different regression *models* (sets of assumptions), some involving stronger conditions than others. (This is a different use of the term *model* than we have seen before. Previously, model referred to the choice of dependent and independent variables.) Not surprisingly, the models with stronger assumptions usually lead to stronger conclusions. A second source of confusion is that the assumptions are typically expressed in mathematical form, making it difficult for many people to understand their practical implications. Finally, there is a tendency to treat all assumptions as equally important when in fact some are much more critical than others.

Actually, we already considered the most important assumptions in Chapter 3, which dealt with major things that can go wrong with multiple regression. That discussion, however, was very informal and incomplete. This chapter deals with the assumptions in a more systematic fashion.

Why have assumptions at all? Like any technique, least squares multiple regression works well in some situations and poorly in others. The assumptions can be thought of as specifying the conditions under which multiple regression works well. Indeed, under some assumptions it can be shown that least squares regression is at least as good as any other method. To talk intelligently about this, we first need to discuss some criteria for deciding whether a statistical technique works well or poorly.

6.1. How Should We Assess the Performance of a Statistical Technique?

The best-known standards of performance for a statistical method are *bias* and *efficiency*. In general, we prefer methods that are *unbiased*. An estimation method is unbiased if there is no systematic tendency to produce estimates that are either too high or too low. Implicit in that statement is the notion that there is a "true" value that we are trying to estimate, and we can either overshoot or undershoot that value. Regardless of the estimation method, once we come up with a particular number as our estimate, we have either an underestimate, an overestimate, or the true value. If a method is unbiased, however, we say that "on average" the overestimates and the underestimates balance out.

It is not enough for a method to be unbiased. You wouldn't be very happy with an unbiased scale that was 10 pounds too high on half of the occasions that it's used and 10 pounds too low the other half. That's where efficiency comes in. Efficiency has to do with how much variation there is around the true value. We measure that variation by the standard error. Efficient estimation methods have standard errors that are as small as possible.

There's one other performance issue that we need to consider. Besides getting estimates, we usually want to test hypotheses or construct confidence intervals. To do this, we (or the computer) need to look things up in a distributional table, typically a normal table, a *t* table, or a chi-square table. If the sample is large, these tables are approximately correct under a very wide range of conditions, but if the sample is small, it may be necessary to make some additional assumptions about the distributions of the variables we are working with.

Now we're ready to consider some assumptions for multiple regression. Essentially, we want to determine the least restrictive set of conditions that would allow us to conclude that multiple regression estimates are unbiased and efficient. In addition, we want to know when the test statistics and confidence intervals are valid. In the remainder of the chapter, I'm going to assume that there is a dependent variable y and two independent variables x_1 and x_2. Everything I say will readily extend to cases where there are additional independent variables, but having just two will greatly simplify the algebra.

6.2. What Is the Probability Sampling Model?

The first model we'll consider is a very simple one that takes an agnostic view of causality. It also produces only weak conclusions. Suppose we have a large population with three variables y, x_1, and x_2. If we had data for the entire population, we could use least squares to estimate a regression with y as the dependent variable. Let's represent that hypothetical regression in the entire population as

$$\hat{y} = A + B_1 x_1 + B_2 x_2.$$

Notice that I've used capital A and B to indicate that these are the "true" or population coefficients. Our goal is to get good estimates of these coefficients.

Because we can't afford to study the entire population, we take a *probability sample* with n cases. A probability sample is a sample in which the probability of selecting any possible sample of size n is known or can be calculated. Without going into details, there are basically three types of probability samples: simple random samples, stratified samples, and cluster samples. We can also have various combinations of these three.

For our purposes, it doesn't matter which kind of probability sample we use, as long as *every individual has an equal probability of being chosen*. Once we have such a probability sample, we apply least squares regression to the sample to get

$$\hat{y} = a + b_1 x_1 + b_2 x_2.$$

That's all there is to the model. Under these conditions, it can be proved that a, b_1, and b_2 are unbiased estimates of A, B_1, and B_2, respectively. But that's as far as we can go. We can't say anything about standard errors or hypothesis tests without introducing stronger assumptions.

The important point here is that least squares regression applied to a probability sample gives reasonable estimates of the least squares regression equation in the population. That shouldn't be terribly surprising—we use the same principle in estimating means and variances. But that leaves us with a critical question: Is the least squares regression equation for the population something worth estimating? Does it really tell us anything fundamental about the causal relationships among the variables in the equation? To answer that question, we have to shift to a different kind of model, one that directly specifies the process generating the dependent variable.

6.3. What Is the Standard Linear Model?

The next model we'll consider is one that is commonly described in most textbooks on regression (e.g., Chatterjee & Price, 1991; Draper & Smith, 1998; Fox, 1997; Kleinbaum, Kupper, Muller, & Nizam, 1998; McClendon, 1994; Mendenhall & Sincich, 1996). Unlike the probability sampling model, this one says nothing about the relationship between a sample and a population. Instead, we presume that we have data on a set of individuals, labeled $i = 1, \ldots, n$, with measurements on variables y, x_1, and x_2. Then we make some assumptions about how values of y are produced from the values of the x's. Although these assumptions are usually expressed in the form of equations, they embody implicit notions of causal effects of the x's on y. I'll briefly present all five assumptions now and then elaborate on each one of them at some length.

1. Linearity. The dependent variable y is a linear function of the x's, plus a *random disturbance* U:

$$y = A + B_1 x_1 + B_2 x_2 + U.$$

What's new here is the disturbance term U. It can be interpreted as a kind of *random noise* that disturbs the relationship between the x's and y. It can also be interpreted as the combined effects of all the causes of y that are not directly included in the equation. Unless we put some restrictions on U, this equation really doesn't say much, so all the remaining assumptions have to do with U.

2. Mean independence. The most important assumption we make about U is that its mean, or average value, does not depend on the x's. More specifically, we assume that the mean of U is always 0.

3. Homoscedasticity (variance independence). The variance of U cannot depend on the x's. It's always the same value, denoted by σ^2.

4. Uncorrelated disturbances. The value of U for any individual in the sample is uncorrelated with the value of U for any other individual.

5. Normal disturbance. U has a normal distribution.

Before examining these assumptions in detail, let's first see what they imply in terms of the performance of least squares.

- Assumptions 1 and 2 guarantee that the least squares estimates a, b_1, and b_2 are unbiased estimates of A, B_1, and B_2, respectively. That's the same result we got from the probability sampling model.
- If we add Assumptions 3 and 4, we find that least squares coefficients are efficient. They have standard errors that are at least as small as those produced by any other unbiased, linear estimation method. This result is captured by the acronym BLUE, which stands for Best Linear Unbiased Estimation method.
- Combined with the other assumptions, the normality assumption (5) implies that a t table can be used validly to calculate p values and confidence intervals.

Now that we've covered the main points of the model, let's look at each of these assumptions in greater detail.

6.4. What Does the Linearity Assumption Mean?

The linear equation in the first assumption tells us how values of y are generated. This equation can be thought of as representing a causal mechanism that can't be directly observed. In particular, the coefficients A, B_1, and B_2 are the "true" parameters that describe that causal mechanism. Our goal is to get good estimates of these parameters.

In thinking about this equation, there are a couple points to remember from Chapter 1. First, we recognize that in most applications of multiple regression, the assumption of linearity will be only approximately true. Second, the form of this equation actually accommodates a wide range of nonlinear relationships that can be introduced by performing some kind of transformation on the x variables.

The disturbance term U is treated as a random variable. Roughly speaking, that means that U has a probability distribution—for every possible value of U, there's a certain probability that that value will occur. Assumption 5 says that the probability distribution is normal, but it could possibly be something else. It's important to realize that there is a different U for each individual in the data set. Potentially, these could have different probability distributions with different means and variances, but the rest of the assumptions impose considerable uniformity on these distributions.

6.5. What Is Mean Independence?

The assumption of mean independence is a way of saying that the x's are unrelated to the random disturbance U. A stronger assumption would be to say that the x's are *independent* of U, but we don't need an assumption that strong. A weaker assumption is that the x's are uncorrelated with U, but that's not quite strong enough to give us the standard results. We assume that the mean of U is 0 to get unbiased estimates of the intercept A. If we care only about unbiasedness of the B's, we need only assume that the mean of U is some constant value. In particular, the mean doesn't depend on the x's.

The assumption of mean independence is the most critical assumption of all because

- Violations can produce severe bias in the estimates
- There are often reasons to expect violations
- There's no way to test for violations without additional data.

In Chapter 1, we discussed some possible violations of this assumption. Essentially, there are three conditions that lead to violations.

1. Omitted x variables. All causes of y that are not explicitly measured and put in the model are considered to be part of the U term. If any of these omitted variables is correlated with the measured x's, that will produce a correlation between the x's and U, thereby violating the mean independence assumption.

2. Reverse causation. If y has a causal effect on any of the x's, then U will indirectly affect the x's. Consequently, the mean of U will be related to the x's.

3. Measurement error in the x's. If the x's are measured with error, that error becomes part of the disturbance term U. Because the

measurement error affects the measured value of the x's, then U must also be related to the x's.

If the data are produced by a randomized experiment, these violations are unlikely to occur. The randomization process ensures that the unmeasured characteristics of the subjects are not related to the treatment variable. Randomization also prevents the dependent variable from affecting the treatment variable.

If you have non-experimental data, violations of the mean independence assumption are always a possibility. If the violation results from omission of variables that are included in your data set, then you can easily correct the problem by putting those variables in your regression equation. In all other cases, there's nothing in the data that will enable you to determine whether or not such violations are present. The only thing you have to go on is your knowledge of the phenomenon you're studying.

As with any statistical assumptions, violations and their consequences are always a matter of degree. A small amount of measurement error in an x variable will produce a small amount of bias in its coefficient. Strong effects of y on the x's will produce large biases in their coefficients.

There are ways of dealing with violations of the mean independence assumption, but they invariably require additional data, additional assumptions, and more complex methods of analysis. For example, biases resulting from measurement error can be corrected if you have external knowledge of the reliability of the variable in question or if you can get multiple indicators of that variable (Hayduk, 1988). In either case, you'll need a special program to incorporate the additional information. For reverse causation, there are *simultaneous equations* methods that are widely used by economists (Greene, 1997; Gujarati, 1995). To use these methods, however, you have to make assumptions that are often as dubious as the assumption of mean independence.

6.6. What Is Homoscedasticity?

The word *homoscedasticity* is derived from a Latin phrase meaning "same variance." The opposite of homoscedasticity is heteroscedasticity. Heteroscedasticity means that the degree of random

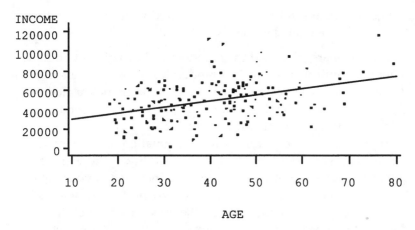

Figure 6.1. Regression of Income on Age With Homoscedasticity

noise in the linear equation varies with the values of the x variables. Homoscedasticity means that the degree of random noise is always the same, regardless of the values of the x variables.

To understand the difference between homo- and heteroscedasticity, there's no substitute for pictures. Figure 6.1 shows a linear regression of income on age for data that were generated under the homoscedasticity assumption. It is apparent that the degree of scatter around the regression line is roughly the same at all ages. There may seem to be a little more variation around age 40 and a little less around age 70, but that's merely an artifact of the greater concentration of people in the middle age levels.

In Figure 6.2, we see a very similar regression line with strong *hetero*scedasticity. The range of variation is very narrow around age 20 but steadily increases with age. The pattern in Figure 6.2 is fairly common for variables like income that are always greater than zero, but heteroscedasticity can come in many other patterns. There could be more variation at lower ages and less variation at higher ages, or the variation could be small at each end and wide in the middle. Anything that departs from a uniform degree of scatter qualifies as heteroscedasticity.

Unlike the assumption of mean independence, the homoscedasticity assumption can be checked readily with the data. For bivariate regression, scatterplots like those in Figure 6.2 can be very informative. For multiple regression, comparable graphs can be produced by plotting the observed value y on the vertical axis and

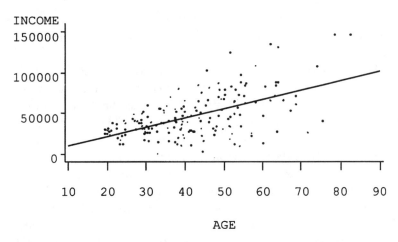

Figure 6.2. Regression of Income on Age With Heteroscedasticity

the predicted value on the horizontal axis. Some regression applications can also perform statistical tests that diagnose the presence of heteroscedasticity.

By itself, heteroscedasticity does not produce any bias in the coefficient estimates, but it does have two notable consequences:

- *Inefficiency*. Least squares estimates no longer have minimum standard errors. That means you can do better using alternative methods. The reason ordinary least squares is not optimal when there is heteroscedasticity is that it gives equal weight to all observations when, in fact, observations with larger disturbance variance contain less information than observations with smaller disturbance variance. The solution is a method known as *weighted least squares* that puts greater weight on the observations with smaller disturbance variance (Gujarati, 1995). Many multiple regression programs will do weighted least squares as an option, but there are too many details for us to consider them here.

- *Biased standard errors*. The standard errors reported by regression programs are only *estimates* of the true standard errors, which cannot be observed directly. If there is heteroscedasticity, these standard error estimates can be seriously biased. That in turn leads to bias in test statistics and confidence intervals.

Of the two problems, bias in the standard errors is more serious because it's more likely to lead to incorrect conclusions. The weighted least squares method can also correct this problem, but a much simpler solution is to use *robust standard errors* that are available as an option in some regression applications. This doesn't change the coefficient estimates and, therefore, doesn't solve the inefficiency problem, but at least the test statistics will give you reasonably accurate p values. An advantage of this approach over weighted least squares is that it requires fewer assumptions.

Another method that is often used for reducing heteroscedasticity is to transform the dependent variable (Mendenhall & Sincich, 1996). For example, instead of using income as the dependent variable, you could use the logarithm of income. This new dependent variable tends to have much less heteroscedasticity than income itself. If the dependent variable is a count of something, like the number of quarrels that a married couple reports in a month, the square root transformation is sometimes recommended. Such transformations are called *variance stabilizing transformations*. The problem with this approach is that it fundamentally changes the nature of the relationship between the dependent variable and the independent variables. As a result, it can make the coefficients more difficult to interpret. If you don't mind that, variance stabilizing transformations can be a simple and effective solution.

My own experience with heteroscedasticity is that it has to be pretty severe before it leads to serious bias in the standard errors. Although it's certainly worth checking, I wouldn't get overly anxious about it.

6.7. What Are Uncorrelated Disturbances?

As I mentioned earlier, the disturbance term U in the linear equation is actually a different random variable for every individual in the sample. Assumption 4 says that the disturbance variables for any two individuals must be uncorrelated. The best way to understand this assumption is to think about how it might be violated. Remember that U can be thought of as containing all the unmeasured variables that affect the dependent variable y. If one of those unmeasured variables is something that two individuals have in common, the result could be a correlation between their U terms. Suppose, for example, that we have a sample of 200 people obtained by interviewing 100 married couples. The dependent variable is a measure of satisfaction with one's neighborhood. Because the husband and wife will, in the vast majority of cases, share the same neighborhood with all its characteristics, we would certainly expect their disturbance terms to be correlated.

Another way that disturbance terms can be correlated is if the behavior of one person in the sample actually affects the behavior of another person in the same sample. Suppose the sample consists of students in a single high school, and the dependent variable is a measure of educational aspirations. In that case, it's quite plausible that students who are at the top of the social hierarchy will have some impact on the aspirations of those lower down.

The most serious cases of correlated disturbances are likely to arise when the same individuals are measured at multiple points in time. Some panel surveys, for example, interview a sample of people every year for several years in a row, asking them pretty much the same questions each time. As you might expect, people's answers to the same questions are often very highly correlated from one year to the next.

More generally, the issue of correlated disturbances is strongly affected by the sampling design. If we have a simple random sample from a large population, it's unlikely that correlated disturbances will be a problem. The probability that any two individuals in the sample will interact or share a common environment will be small. On the other hand, if the sampling method involves any kind of clustering, where people are chosen in groups rather than as individuals, the possibility of correlated disturbances should be seriously considered.

The general consequences of correlated disturbances are identical to those for heteroscedasticity. Although the coefficients remain unbiased, they will be inefficient—least squares is no longer the optimal method. More seriously, the estimated standard errors will be biased. With heteroscedasticity, the direction of the bias in the standard errors is hard to predict. With correlated disturbances, however, the standard errors are almost always biased downward. That means that the coefficients are less accurately measured than you think they are. It also implies that the test statistics will be biased upward. As a result, there will be a tendency to conclude that relationships exist when they really don't.

Although it is possible to diagnose correlated disturbances by examining the data, there aren't many convenient ways to do it. If the data come in pairs, as with husbands and wives, you can calculate the residuals from the regression and then compute the correlations between husbands' and wives' residuals for the sample of married couples. For more general forms of clustering, the natural statistic to examine would be something called the *intraclass correla-*

tion coefficient (Haggard, 1958), but there are few statistical packages that will calculate it without special programming.

Solutions to the problem of correlated disturbances are quite similar to those for heteroscedasticity. The method of *generalized least squares* will produce optimal estimates of the coefficients and good estimates of the standard errors (Greene, 1997). Unfortunately, generalized least squares is rarely available in standard regression applications. Special programs are necessary, and those programs can be rather complex to use. A simpler approach is to stick with the least squares coefficients but use robust standard errors. Although these standard errors are not currently available in most regression programs, I expect that many applications will add them in the coming years.

6.8. What Is the Normality Assumption?

Much confusion exists about the normality assumption for multiple regression. Many people think that *all* the variables in a regression equation must be normally distributed. Nothing could be further from the truth. The only variable that is assumed to have a normal distribution is the disturbance term U, which is something we can't observe directly. The x variables can have any kind of distribution. Because y is a linear function of both the x's and U, there's no requirement that y be normally distributed either.

Another thing to keep in mind about the normality assumption is that it's probably the least important of the five assumptions. The criteria of unbiasedness and efficiency don't depend at all on this assumption. If the sample is moderately large, we can dispense with the normality assumption entirely. When the sample is small, we need normality of the disturbance term to guarantee that confidence intervals and p values will be accurate, but as the sample gets larger, the *central limit theorem* tells us that these statistics will be good approximations even if U is not normally distributed. How large does the sample have to be for the central limit theorem to apply? That depends on such things as the actual distribution of U and the number of independent variables in the regression equation, but I usually feel comfortable with anything more than 200 cases. Even 100 is probably OK in most circumstances if the number of x variables is small, say less than five.

When you get below 100 cases in the sample, the normality assumption becomes more critical. The natural way to check this assumption is to calculate the residuals from the regression and see if they follow something like a normal distribution. There are well-known tests for determining whether a variable has a normal distribution. Unfortunately, these tests tend to be unreliable in small samples, and that's exactly when you need them.

My advice is to be more conservative in the use and interpretation of p values when the sample is small, to compensate for the possibility that the computed p values may only be rough approximations. If you want to avoid Type I errors (concluding that a variable has an effect when it really doesn't), insist on p values that are smaller than the standard criteria. For example, instead of concluding that a coefficient is significant when the p value is less than .05, do so only when the p value is less than .01. Many researchers do exactly the opposite, however. They use less stringent criteria in small samples than in large samples because it's harder to find significant effects in small samples. In my view, this is a dangerous practice.

6.9. Are There Any Other Assumptions for Multiple Regression?

In some textbooks, you'll find the additional assumption that the x variables are *fixed* rather than random. This means that the values of the x variables don't change from one sample to another. If gender is one of your variables and you have 150 males and 175 females in your sample, the fixed-x condition would require that every possible sample have exactly 150 males and 175 females. This condition is almost never satisfied in non-experimental research. In any kind of practical probability sampling design, the exact distribution of the x variables will vary substantially from one sample to another. The fixed-x condition *can* be satisfied in experimental research because the researcher has control over how many cases fall into each treatment category.

Fortunately, the fixed-x assumption is completely unnecessary. All the standard properties of least squares estimates can be derived without invoking it. So why make this assumption? The main reason is that it greatly simplifies the algebra necessary to prove the properties of least squares. Because we're accepting those results on faith in this book, there's no need to consider this assumption.

Some textbooks also include the assumption that there is no perfect multicollinearity among the x variables. (An equivalent but obscure way of expressing this condition is to say that the X matrix has full rank.) Although this is certainly a necessary condition for computing linear regression estimates, it's really a property of the sample rather than the population or the underlying mechanism generating the data. For that reason, I do not include it in the assumptions, but I do consider multicollinearity in some detail in Chapter 7.

As I mentioned at the beginning of the chapter, you will find somewhat different sets of assumptions discussed in different textbooks. One set of assumptions is the *multivariate normal model*. This model says, quite succinctly, that the observed variables have a multivariate normal distribution. Among other things, this means that every variable in the regression equation is normally distributed. Moreover, every variable is linearly related to every other variable, and those linear equations are homoscedastic. The multivariate normal model implies all the assumptions we have considered here, but it's *much* stronger than necessary to derive the standard properties of least squares estimates.

In some discussions of multiple regression, you'll find the mean independence and homoscedasticity assumptions replaced with the single assumption that x and U are independent. Although this simplifies things a bit, it's more restrictive than necessary. Moreover, it obscures the quite different consequences of violating mean independence and violating homoscedasticity.

Chapter Highlights

1. There are several different models (sets of assumptions) that may be used to justify ordinary least squares regression.

2. We want estimation methods that are unbiased, at least approximately. Unbiased methods have no systematic tendency to underestimate or overestimate the true value.

3. Efficient estimation methods have standard errors that are as small as possible. That means that in repeated sampling, they don't fluctuate much around the true value.

4. If we have a probability sample drawn so that every individual in the population has the same chance of being chosen, then the least squares regression in the sample is an unbiased estimate of the least squares regression in the population.

5. The standard linear model has five assumptions about how values of the dependent variable are generated from values of the independent variables. If all these assumptions are met, ordinary least squares has several desirable properties. The assumptions of linearity and mean independence imply that least squares is unbiased. The additional assumptions of homoscedasticity and uncorrelated errors imply that least squares is efficient. The normality assumption implies that a t table gives valid p values for hypothesis tests.

6. The disturbance term U represents all the unmeasured causes of the dependent variable y. It's assumed to be a random variable, having an associated probability distribution.

7. Mean independence means that the mean of the random disturbance U does not depend on the values of the x variables.

8. Mean independence of U is the most critical assumption of the standard linear model because violations can produce severe bias and there are often reasons to suspect that violations will occur.

9. Violations of mean independence will occur if (a) important x variables are omitted from the regression model, (b) y has a causal effect on one or more x's, or (c) the x's are measured with error.

10. Homoscedasticity means that the degree of random noise in the relationship between y and the x's is always the same.

11. A good way to check for violations of the homoscedasticity assumption is to plot the residuals against the predicted values of y. There should be a uniform degree of scatter, regardless of the predicted values.

12. Heteroscedasticity (violation of homoscedasticity) can make ordinary least squares inefficient and can produce bias in standard error estimates.

13. There are three ways to deal with heteroscedasticity: variance stabilizing transformations, weighted least squares, and corrected standard errors. Although sometimes effective in reduc-

ing heteroscedasticity, variance stabilizing transformations often have other undesirable properties.

14. Weighted least squares is a good method for correcting heteroscedasticity if you are confident about the form of the heteroscedasticity. Otherwise, you're better off using corrected standard errors.

15. The assumption of uncorrelated errors is usually satisfied if you have a simple random sample from a large population, but it's likely to be violated if observations are selected in clusters or if sample units can interact with each other.

16. Correlated errors can cause serious underestimates of standard errors, leading to inflated test statistics. This problem can be solved with a method known as generalized least squares.

17. The normality assumption is the least critical of the five assumptions. It has nothing to do with the independent variables, and it can be safely ignored if the sample is large.

Questions to Think About

1. A researcher tells you that he doesn't want to use multiple regression on his data because it requires too many assumptions. What response would you give?

2. An unbiased estimation method is one that "on average" gives the right answer. Because any specific estimate might be very far from the true value, why do we care about unbiasedness?

3. Suppose we have a simple random sample of students currently enrolled in U.S. colleges. In the sample, we regress GPA on SAT scores, parents' annual income, and hours per week spent studying. What does this regression tell us, if anything, about the complete population of students?

4. Every regression program produces both coefficients and standard errors. What do the standard errors mean? Why do we want them to be small?

5. The first assumption in the standard linear model is that y is a linear function of the x's, plus a random disturbance term U. I claimed that "unless we put some restrictions on U, this equation really doesn't say much." Why does the linearity assumption have little content unless restrictions are placed on U?

6. Chapter 3 states that when "important" variables are omitted from a regression equation, the coefficients of the included variables will be biased. How does the omission of variables lead to a violation of the mean independence assumption?

7. Dr. Hamilton published the results of a multiple regression showing that certain parenting styles lead to higher rates of juvenile delinquency. A critic claims that Hamilton should have checked whether his data satisfy the mean independence assumption. What answer should he give?

8. In later checking, Hamilton's student discovered that there was a substantial amount of heteroscedasticity in the regression of juvenile delinquency on parenting styles. Does this mean Hamilton's published results were invalid? What should he be concerned about, if anything?

9. Professor Long does a regression in which the units of analysis are the 50 U.S. states. Her dependent variable is a measure of support for environmental legislation, and her principal independent variable is the percentage of the state's economy devoted to manufacturing. Should she be concerned about the possibility of correlated errors? Why or why not?

10. Many regression analysts use dummy variables as independent variables, but dummy variables cannot possibly be normally distributed. Is this a problem for regression analysis?

11. For a sample of 5,000 discharged military personnel, Dr. Short wants to do a regression analysis of length of service on several independent variables. Length of service is highly skewed—not at all like a normal distribution. Can he go ahead with the regression analysis?

7 What Can Be Done About Multicollinearity?

Multicollinearity is something that nearly all users of multiple regression have heard about. Unfortunately, their knowledge of multicollinearity is often limited to two facts:

- It's bad.
- It has something to do with high correlations among the variables.

Beyond those truths, there is an enormous amount of confusion and mythology surrounding multicollinearity. This chapter will set you straight.

7.1. What Is Extreme Multicollinearity?

Multicollinearity comes in two forms: extreme and near-extreme. Extreme multicollinearity means that at least two of the independent variables in a regression equation are perfectly related by a linear function. Suppose you're trying to estimate the model

$$y = A + B_1x_1 + B_2x_2 + B_3x_3 + U.$$

Suppose that in your sample, it happens to be the case that

$$x_1 = 2 + 3x_2.$$

Notice that there is no error term in this equation. Then the correlation between x_1 and x_2 is 1.0 and we have a case of extreme multicollinearity.

The consequence of extreme multicollinearity is simple: It's impossible to get separate estimates for the coefficients B_1 and B_2. If you try to do it anyway, the computer will do one of two things:

- Print an error message but no results.
- Arbitrarily pick either x_1 or x_2, throw that variable out of the model, and estimate the model with the remaining variables. Usually, a warning message is also printed.

Box 7.1 is an example of the output from SPSS when the two independent variables are perfectly correlated.

BOX 7.1. Excluded Variable[b]

Model	Beta In	t	Sig.	Partial Correlation	Collinearity Statistics Tolerance
1 X2	a.	.	.	.	.000

a. Predictors in the Model: (Constant), X1
b. Dependent Variable: Time (months)

After reporting the results from the regression on x_1, we are told that x_2 has been excluded from the regression model. The tolerance is a useful statistic that we'll look at a bit later.

Box 7.2 is an example of a warning message produced by the SAS® System.

BOX 7.2

```
NOTE: Model is not full rank. Least-squares
solutions for the parameters are not unique. Some
statistics will be misleading. A reported DF of 0
or B means that the estimate is biased.
   The following parameters have been set to 0,
since the variables are a linear combination of
other variables as shown.

X1 = +2.0000 * INTERCEP +3.0000 * X2
```

The statement "Model is not full rank" is equivalent to saying that there is extreme multicollinearity. In this case, the variable x_2 is a perfect linear function of the variable x_1. The program excluded x_2

from the model because it happened to be the second variable listed on the model specification.

Why does this happen? Remember that multiple regression is trying to separate out the effects of two or more variables, even though they are correlated with each other. To do this, however, there must be some remaining variation on each x variable when the other x variables are held constant. If two variables are perfectly correlated, when you hold one constant, the other must be constant as well. Hence, it's impossible to separate their effects on the dependent variable. (It might be helpful to reread Section 6.5 and think about what would happen if x_1 and x_2 were perfectly correlated.)

Extreme multicollinearity is unusual in the social sciences, but it does happen. When it occurs, it's usually because of some artifact in the way the independent variables are constructed. For example, suppose you ask people to estimate the percentage of information about current events they get from (a) television, (b) radio, (c) print media, and (d) conversations with others. Respondents are told that the percentages must sum to 100. Let x_1 through x_4 be variables containing the four percentages. If you tried to use all four of these as independent variables in a multiple regression, you would have extreme multicollinearity. Because they always add up to 100, any one of them can be expressed as a linear function of the other three. For instance, we can write $x_4 = 100 - x_1 - x_2 - x_3$. This sort of problem often occurs with sets of dummy variables, as I'll explain in the next chapter.

What can be done about extreme multicollinearity? For the variables that are collinear with each other, the answer is nothing. There's simply no way to get distinct coefficient estimates for them. What is essential to remember is that *multicollinearity only affects the coefficient estimates for those variables that are collinear*. This is true for both extreme and near-extreme multicollinearity. If x_1 and x_2 are perfectly correlated but x_3 is uncorrelated with either of them, then there's no difficulty in getting estimates for the effect of x_3 controlling for the other two variables. The way to do it is what many regression programs do automatically: arbitrarily pick either x_1 or x_2 and remove it from the equation. Then the estimated coefficient for x_3 is OK. The estimated coefficient for, say, x_1 represents the combined effect of x_1 and x_2, so you must be cautious in interpreting it.

7.2. What Is Near-Extreme Multicollinearity?

The one good thing about extreme multicollinearity is that you can't miss it. By contrast, the much more common problem of near-extreme multicollinearity is more insidious. It can cause you to make seriously incorrect conclusions without you being aware of the problem.

Near-extreme multicollinearity means simply that there are strong (but not perfect) linear relationships among the independent variables. If the regression model has only two independent variables, near-extreme multicollinearity occurs if the two variables have a correlation that's close to 1 or –1. How close does it have to be? Like everything else in regression, it's a matter of degree. The closer you get to 1 or –1, the greater the associated problems.

It's a little more difficult to describe near-extreme multicollinearity when there are three or more variables that are collinear. Suppose you have three independent variables, x_1, x_2, and x_3. Pick one of them, say x_2, and regress it on x_1 and x_3. If the R^2 from that regression is near 1, then x_2 is collinear with x_1 and x_3. It's worth remembering that multicollinearity has nothing to do with the dependent variable— it's a characteristic of the relationships among the independent variables.

Near-extreme multicollinearity does not prevent calculation of the regression coefficients. It does make it more difficult to reliably estimate the coefficients of those variables that are collinear. This can cause a number of difficulties that are described in Section 7.4. First, however, we'll look at some methods for diagnosing the existence of near-extreme multicollinearity. In the remainder of this chapter, when I use the word "multicollinearity," you can assume I'm referring to the near-extreme case.

7.3. How Can Multicollinearity Be Diagnosed?

The old-fashioned way to check for multicollinearity is to examine the matrix of two-variable correlations among all the independent variables. Most statistical packages can produce such a matrix. If any of the correlations is very high (near 1 or –1), we conclude that multicollinearity is a problem.

The disadvantage of this method is that it's quite possible that *none* of the bivariate correlations may be very high, yet multicollinearity could still be serious. Consider the following correlation matrix for four independent variables:

	x_1	x_2	x_3	x_4
x_1	1.00			
x_2	.10	1.00		
x_3	.10	.10	1.00	
x_4	.60	.50	.60	1.00

Examined one by one, none of these correlations is so large as to cause major concern, but if we regress x_4 on the other three x variables, we get an R^2 of .81, high enough to qualify as serious multicollinearity by almost anyone's standards. This is, in fact, a good way of diagnosing multicollinearity: Regress each independent variable on all the other *independent* variables, and look for a high R^2 in any of these regressions. How high is high? Personally, I start to get concerned when any of these R^2s is above .60 or so.

Some regression programs will automatically produce these diagnostic R^2s if you request them. Actually, what they give you is usually something called a *tolerance*, which is 1 minus the R^2 for each independent variable. (Why they subtract the R^2s from 1, I don't know.) You want to watch out for low tolerances. Consistent with my standard for the R^2, I start to worry when any of the tolerances is below .40.

Another equivalent multicollinearity diagnostic that may be reported for each independent variable is something called the *variance inflation factor*. This is just the reciprocal of the tolerance (1/tolerance). I'll explain the reason for this name in the next section. Tolerances below .40 correspond to variance inflation factors above 2.50.

Here are the tolerances and variance inflation factors for the four variables in the correlation matrix above.

	Tolerance	Variance Inflation Factor
x_1	0.42	2.38
x_2	0.54	1.85
x_3	0.42	2.38
x_4	0.19	5.27

As we already saw, x_4 has serious problems with its low tolerance and high variance inflation factor (VIF). The other three variables have less serious problems, although they're quite close to my personal criterion of .40 for the tolerance and 2.50 for the variance inflation factor.

In addition to these variable-by-variable measures of multicollinearity, some programs will give you more comprehensive statistics that help you determine which variables are linearly related to which other variables. These statistics may be useful in some cases, but they can also be more difficult to interpret than the tolerances or variance inflation factors.

7.4. What Are the Consequences of Multicollinearity?

Near-extreme multicollinearity is *not* a violation of any of the assumptions we discussed in Chapter 6. As long as the assumptions in Section 6.3 are satisfied, the least squares estimates are still BLUE (best linear unbiased estimates). So what's the problem? If an independent variable is highly collinear with other variables, the standard error of its coefficient will be large. This fact is captured by the variance inflation factor described in the last section. The square root of the variance inflation factor tells you how much larger the standard error is, compared with what it would be if that variable were uncorrelated with the other x variables in the equation. In the previous section, the variance inflation factor for x_4 was 5.27, which has a square root of 2.3. This means that the standard error for the coefficient of x_4 is 2.3 times as large as it would be if x_4 were uncorrelated with the other xs. It follows that the confidence interval around the coefficient will be more than twice as wide as if there were no multicollinearity, and the t statistic will be less than half as large.

So one big problem with multicollinearity is that it's harder to find statistically significant coefficients. Keep in mind that that statement applies only to the variables with high variance inflation factors. The variables with low variance inflation factors are unaffected. For the variables that are collinear, however, the inflation of the standard errors—although an accurate reflection of uncertainty—can produce quite misleading conclusions.

Here's a simple example. Suppose we interview a sample of 150 newlywed women and we ask them how many children they want (x_1) and their number of years of schooling (x_2). One year later, we again ask them how many children they want (x_3). Five years later, we find out how many children they actually have (y). We then regress y on x_1, x_2, and x_3. The correlation matrix for the four variables is

	x_1	x_2	x_3	y
x_1	1.00			
x_2	−.15	1.00		
x_3	.90	−.20	1.00	
y	.35	−.23	.37	1.00

Notice the correlation of .90 between x_1 and x_3, the two measures of number of desired children.

If we regress y on all three x variables, we get the following standardized coefficients, t statistics, and variance inflation factors.

	Coefficient	t Statistic	VIF
x_1	0.12	0.67	5.29
x_2	−0.17	−2.15	1.05
x_3	0.23	1.33	5.39

Because the t statistic for schooling (x_2) is above 2 in magnitude, we conclude that it has a significant, negative impact on number of children. However, neither of the two measures of desired number of children has a significant effect on actual number of children.

But look what happens when we delete x_3 from the model:

	Coefficient	t Statistic	VIF
x_1	0.32	4.21	1.02
x_2	−0.18	−2.37	1.02

The coefficient for x_1 has nearly tripled, and the t statistic has increased to 4.21, which has a p value less than .0001. Similar results occur when x_1 is deleted from the model:

	Coefficient	t Statistic	VIF
x_2	−0.16	−2.11	1.04
x_3	0.34	4.38	1.04

What does this tell us? Clearly there is an important relationship between desired number of children and actual number of children, but that relationship is obscured when we put two highly correlated measures of desired number of children in the same model. When we hold constant the desired number of children at time 1, there's so little remaining variation in desired number of children at time 2 that we can't get reliable estimates for that variable. The same thing happens when we control for the time 2 measure. Either of the reduced regressions therefore gives a more accurate picture than the regression that includes all three x variables.

There's something else to be learned from the regression with all three x variables. Notice that in the correlation matrix, the correlation between x_1 and y is .35, and the correlation between x_3 and y is .37. There is not much of a difference. When we put both variables in the same regression, however, the standardized coefficient for x_1 is .12 and the standardized coefficient for x_3 is .23. That is a big difference. This phenomenon is known as the *tipping effect*. The general principle is that when independent variables are highly correlated, small differences in their bivariate relationships with the dependent variable get magnified into large differences in the regression coefficients.

The difference between a correlation of .35 and a correlation of .37 is so small that it could easily arise from tiny changes in the data. Sampling errors, measurement errors, coding errors, missing data—any of these could easily produce a difference of that magnitude. Yet, as we've just seen, such small changes can lead to major differences in the magnitudes of the coefficients. This example points out the instability of regression coefficients under conditions of multicollinearity. In general, multicollinearity makes multiple regression much more sensitive to minor errors or departures from the assumptions of the model. In other words, the coefficients are less *robust*.

One manifestation of these problems is that the coefficients for variables that are collinear are often surprising or counterintuitive. Coefficients that you feel confident ought to be positive turn out to be negative. Standardized coefficients may be greater than 1.0 in magnitude. These are both common symptoms of multicollinearity. Even when such "strange" coefficients are statistically significant, you should be wary about placing too much importance on them.

As with many other problems we've discussed, multicollinearity is only a minor concern for models whose primary goal is prediction. Suppose you estimate a model with an R^2 of .85, which is pretty good for a predictive model. Then you add another independent variable that has a correlation of .90 with one of the variables already in the model. The R^2 will hardly change at all, and neither will the actual predicted values. The standard errors of the predicted values may increase a bit, so there is some disadvantage of adding redundant variables to prediction models.

7.5. Are There Situations in Which Multicollinearity Is More Likely to Occur?

Certain kinds of data are particularly prone to multicollinearity. One is time-series data. In the classic time-series design, there is a single case that is observed at many points in time. For example, the case could be the U.S. economy measured at quarterly intervals over a period of 40 years. The variables might include GNP, unemployment rate, inflation rate, and so on. With time-series data, there is a tendency for variables to be highly correlated. One reason is that there are consistent long-term trends in many different variables.

Another common over-time design is the panel study. In this design, many cases are observed at two or more points in time. For example, a sample of 1,000 people may be interviewed annually over a period of 5 years. Although this kind of data is less prone to multicollinearity than the classic time-series design, most variables tend to be highly correlated with themselves at earlier or later points in time. We saw this in the example in Section 7.4, where desired number of children at time 1 was highly correlated with desired number of children at time 2.

A rather different kind of data is variously known as *aggregated*, *group-level*, or *ecological* data. With data of this sort, the units of analysis are groups of individuals, and the variables are summary measures of individual characteristics. Here's a real example. In a study designed to explain homicide rates among Black males (Phillips, 1997), data were collected for 222 metropolitan areas in the United States. In each city, the following variables were measured in 1990:

BHOM: Black homicide rate

BFEMHEAD: Percentage of Black households headed by females

BLFP: Percentage of Blacks in the labor force

BPOVERTY: Percentage of Black households below the poverty line

INEQ: Inequality of Black incomes

TABLE 7.1 Correlations Among Five Characteristics of U.S. Metropolitan
Areas

Variable	BHOM	BFEMHEAD	BLFP	BPOVERTY	INEQ
BHOM	1.00				
BFEMHEAD	0.17	1.00			
BLFP	-0.20	-0.45	1.00		
BPOVERTY	0.20	0.56	-0.70	1.00	
INEQ	0.30	0.59	-0.51	0.66	1.00

Table 7.1 gives the correlations among these variables. Although the
correlations between the homicide rate and the other four variables
are only moderately high, the remaining correlations are all quite
substantial.

Why are such high correlations common with aggregate data?
Although there's no definitive answer to this question, the most
plausible explanation is that random variation among individual
people tends to average out when they are combined into groups.
This phenomenon is a double-edged sword, however. You can often
get very high R^2 for aggregate data, but it may be quite difficult to
get reliable estimates of the coefficients because of multicollinearity.

Table 7.2 shows the results of regressing the homicide rate on the
other four variables. Only one of the variables, Inequality of Black
incomes, is statistically significant: Greater inequality is associated
with a higher homicide rate. Note that the tolerances for all the
variables are on the low side, with one of them (BPOVERTY) below
.40. This should raise questions as to how much confidence to put
in the results.

TABLE 7.2 Regression of Black Male Homicide Rate on Characteristics of
Metropolitan Areas

Variable	Coefficient	t	p	Tolerance	Variance Inflation Factor
BFEMHEAD	-0.02	-0.15	0.88	.60	1.67
BLFP	-0.19	-1.05	0.29	.51	1.97
BPOVERTY	-0.08	-0.42	0.68	.37	2.67
INEQ	1.12	-3.14	0.002	.50	2.02

7.6. Are There Any Solutions?

There are a lot of options for dealing with near-extreme multi-collinearity, but all of them are flawed in one way or another. The fundamental problem is that there isn't enough information in the data to separate out the effects of the collinear variables. No technical fix can adequately compensate for that lack of information.

In thinking about solutions, we need to distinguish two rather different situations:

- The collinear variables are conceptually distinct
- The collinear variables can be seen as alternative measures of the same conceptual variable

The case of alternative measures is much easier to deal with. For this case, there are four common solutions.

1. *Delete one or more variables from the model.* Recall the example in Section 7.4 in which we had two measures of desired number of children, taken 1 year apart, with a correlation of .90. A natural reaction to this example would be to say "Why put both variables in the model? They're obviously both measuring a stable phenomenon, so there's no point in trying to get separate estimates of each one controlling for the other." But which one do you eliminate? With a correlation that high, it really doesn't make much difference. The time 2 measure has a higher correlation with the dependent variable, so that's a point in its favor. On the other hand, the time 1 measure has the virtue of being unaffected by births in the first year.

2. *Combine the collinear variables into an index.* Deleting variables may be less attractive when the variables have lower correlations with one another. If the two measures of desired number of children had a correlation of .80 instead of .90, it might seem like something important is being lost by deleting one of them. One way to resolve that problem is to combine the two (or more) variables into a single variable, called an index. There are lots of different ways to do this, some simple, some complex. If the variables have the same units of measurement, a simple sum or average may suffice. If they have different units of measurement, it's better to average the *standardized scores* (subtract the mean and divide by the standard deviation).

3. *Estimate a latent variable model.* Instead of creating an index, some researchers take the ultimate step and estimate a latent variable model. Such models assume that there is a single, unobserved

variable that affects the two or more observed variables that are collinear. The models require specialized software and are rather complex, both conceptually and operationally (Hayduk, 1988). The main advantages are that (a) the method corrects for measurement error, thereby solving one of the problems we discussed in Chapter 6, and (b) the method impresses some people with its sophistication.

4. *Perform joint hypothesis tests.* There is another simple method that can be used to great advantage when you want to leave the original, collinear variables in the regression equation. As we saw in the examples in Section 7.4, the most serious danger of multicollinearity is concluding that none of the collinear variables has an effect on the dependent variable when, in fact, any one of them alone has a very strong effect. Instead of looking at the test statistics and *p* values for each variable, you can test the joint hypothesis that "none of the collinear variables has a coefficient that differs from zero." Many regression programs have options for testing hypotheses like this. In the example of desired number of children, the two collinear variables, x_1 and x_3, had individual *p* values of .44 and .13 when both variables were in the equation. When I ran a test of the hypothesis that both variables had a coefficient of 0, however, the *p* value was .007, indicating a clear rejection of the null hypothesis. In the Black homicide example (Table 7.2), there were three variables in the regression whose coefficients were not statistically significant. When I did a joint test for all three coefficients, the *p* value was .76, indicating that the conclusions were robust to the multicollinearity.

What about situations in which the collinear variables are conceptually distinct? Suppose, for example, that we want to estimate a model predicting children's academic performance. Two of the independent variables—hours per day doing homework and hours per day watching TV—have a correlation of −.80. What should we do? It's not surprising that these two variables are highly correlated, but one can imagine quite different causal mechanisms by which they affect academic performance. They're clearly not measuring exactly the same thing, so we probably wouldn't want to combine them into an index or estimate a latent variable model. Unfortunately, if the aim is to get distinct, reliable estimates of the coefficients for these two variables, there's not much that can be done with collinear data. The best I can advise is to experiment with deleting variables and performing joint hypothesis tests. At least this will help you avoid the error of concluding that neither of the variables is important, but it doesn't accomplish the goal of getting distinct estimates.

The only real solution to the problem of multicollinearity is to get better data. Simply increasing the sample size can help a great deal. Although it may not remove the multicollinearity, a larger sample will reduce the inflated standard errors that stem from multicollinearity. Even better is to somehow get data in which the variables are not collinear. Instead of aggregate data, use individual-level data. Instead of time-series data, use cross-sectional data. Stratified sampling on the independent variables can also help reduce the multicollinearity. Of course, this is all easier said than done. Acquiring new data can be time-consuming and expensive, and there is no guarantee that the new data will be any less problematic than the old.

Chapter Highlights

1. Extreme multicollinearity occurs when an independent variable in a linear regression model is a perfect linear function of other independent variables. Regression estimates cannot be computed when there is extreme multicollinearity. Most regression programs exclude one or more of the variables to produce regression estimates.

2. Multicollinearity affects only the coefficient estimates for those variables that are collinear.

3. Near-extreme multicollinearity occurs when there are strong, but not perfect, linear relationships among the independent variables.

4. The best measure of near-extreme multicollinearity is the tolerance, a number associated with each independent variable. The tolerance is computed by regressing each independent variable on all the other independent variables, then subtracting the R^2 from that regression from 1. A low tolerance means serious multicollinearity.

5. Although multicollinearity does not violate any assumptions of the standard regression model, it does make it difficult to get reliable estimates of the coefficients of the variables that are collinear.

6. When two (or more) independent variables are highly collinear, it can appear that neither of them affects the dependent variable, but when either is excluded from the model, the remaining variable may have a highly significant effect.

7. Multicollinearity makes multiple regression much more sensitive to minor errors or departures from the assumptions of the model.

8. Multicollinearity is not so serious when the main goal of the regression analysis is to predict the dependent variable.

9. Multicollinearity is a common problem with time-series data or with aggregate data.

10. When the collinear variables can be thought of as alternative measures of the same underlying dimensions, there are four common solutions: (a) delete one or more variables, (b) combine the variables into an index, (c) estimate a latent variable model, or (d) perform joint hypothesis tests.

Questions to Think About

1. Professor Miller wants to estimate a regression model predicting attitude toward abortion, using data from the General Social Survey. This national survey is conducted annually, and Miller has a data set that combines results from several different years. He calculated each person's age by subtracting the year of birth from the year of the survey. His regression model includes three variables: respondent's age, respondent's year of birth, and calendar year of the survey. His regression program refuses to produce estimates. What's wrong here?

2. For the regression described in the preceding question, Professor Miller also wants to include years of schooling as an independent variable. Does he need to be concerned about collinearity problems affecting the estimates for this variable?

3. There are 20 other variables that Professor Miller wants to include in his regression analysis. He examines all the two-variable correlations (there are 120 of them) and finds that none is above .40. Can he be confident that multicollinearity is not a problem for these variables? Why or why not?

4. For a sample of recent college graduates, Dr. Harrison performs a regression analysis to study the effect of extracurricular activities in college on starting salary in the first job. Her independent variables include (x_1) number of campus organizations in which the student was a member, (x_2) number of organizations in which the student was an officer, and (x_3) number of hours per week devoted to extracurricular activities. She finds that none of these variables is statistically significant. Is she safe in concluding that extracurriculars have no impact on starting salaries? If not, what should she do?

5. A weather forecaster constructs a regression model to predict the amount of rainfall on a given day based on numerous atmospheric measurements made the previous day. The R^2 for this regression is .85, which is much better than previous models. When he examines multicollinearity diagnostics, however, he finds that several of the independent variables have tolerances less than .30. Should he be concerned about his model? If yes, what should he do?

6. An educational researcher wants to know how use of the Internet affects the grades of high school students. Her dependent variable is GPA. Her independent variables include three time measurements from the previous month: (x_1) hours spent on the Internet, (x_2) hours spent on other on-line services, and (x_3) hours of total computer usage. She finds that x_1 is statistically significant at the .05 level but x_2 and x_3 are not. The tolerance for x_1 is .38. Is she safe in concluding that total computer usage doesn't matter, but time on the Internet does matter?

8   How Can Multiple Regression Handle Nonlinear Relationships?

Although multiple regression is based on a *linear* model, there are many special techniques that make it possible to incorporate a wide range of nonlinear relationships. In this chapter we examine three techniques that are widely used: transformations of variables, dummy variables, and interactions between two or more variables.

8.1. How Can a Linear Model Represent Nonlinear Relationships?

The multiple regression model says that

$$y = A + B_1 x_1 + B_2 x_2 + \ldots + B_k x_k + U.$$

We say that this model is linear but, more precisely, it is linear in the Bs—the regression coefficients. That means that we take each of the Bs, multiply it by some number, and then add the results together. On the other hand, this model does not have to be linear in the xs. We can make any mathematical transformation of the xs without causing any serious difficulty—except, perhaps, difficulty in interpreting the results. So instead of x_1, we could substitute the logarithm of x_1, the square of x_1, or the square root of x_1. There are two reasons why we might want to do such things. First, we may have some theoretical reason for expecting the relationship between an independent variable and the dependent variable to follow a certain mathematical form that does not happen to be linear. Second, graphical examination of the data may suggest that the relationship is better described by a curved path rather than a straight line.

Once you've decided on a particular transformation, the implementation is usually straightforward. Most regression programs have facilities for transforming variables, either by clicking on various options or by writing a simple equation.

8.2. What Transformations Are Used on the Dependent Variable?

In Chapter 6, I discussed the possibility of transforming the dependent variable to alleviate problems with heteroscedasticity. Although transformations may reduce heteroscedasticity, they also fundamentally alter the relationship between the dependent and independent variables. That's usually undesirable. Sometimes, however, the transformed relationship is more appealing than the original, linear relationship.

The most common transformation of the dependent variable is to take its logarithm. This gives us the equation

$$\log y = A + B_1 x_1 + B_2 x_2 + \ldots + B_k x_k + U.$$

Nowadays, logarithms are almost always *natural logarithms*, which means that they use the base e, which is approximately 2.71828. By *exponentiating* both sides of this equation, we get

$$y = exp\ (B_1 x_1 + B_2 x_2 + \ldots + B_k x_k + U).$$

Why would such a model be attractive? There are two related reasons. First, there are some variables, like annual salary or time spent watching TV, that are never negative. The logarithmic transformation guarantees that regardless of the values of the Bs or the xs, the predicted value of y will always be a positive number.

Second, the usual linear model says that the effect of increasing a given x variable by one unit is to produce a certain absolute change in y. The logarithmic model, by contrast, says that the effect of changing the x variable by one unit is to produce a certain *percentage* change in y. This often makes more sense, especially for monetary variables. If we consider the effect of gender on income, for example, which statement do you think is more likely to be a good approximation to the facts: "Women make 20% less than men, regardless of the occupation" or "Women make $10,000 less than men, regardless of the occupation"? Although neither statement is likely to be precisely true, we would certainly expect the dollar disparity to be

greater in high-salaried occupations than in low-salaried occupations. That means that the percentage statement should be more
accurate, in general.

As an example, I took the logarithm of income for the data in
Table 1.1. Using SPSS, this was accomplished by the transformation

$$loginc = LN(income)$$

where LN stands for natural logarithm. I then specified a model with
loginc as the dependent variable and schooling and age as independent variables. The least squares estimates are

$$loginc = 7.58 +.094 \text{ schooling} +.025 \text{ age} \qquad R^2 = .26$$
$$(t = 2.44) \qquad (t = 2.65)$$

These results are similar to those we got for the strictly linear model,
which had an R^2 of .28 and t statistics of 2.86 and 2.42. In terms of
model fit, there's no apparent reason to prefer the logarithmic model
to the linear model.

If you run a model like this, there's a simple transformation of
the coefficients that converts them into percentage changes. If the
estimated coefficient of x is b, use a hand calculator to get

$$100(e^b - 1).$$

This gives you the percentage change in y for a one-unit increase in
x. For the two coefficients in the loginc equation above, we get

$$100(e^{.094} - 1) = 9.9\%$$
$$100(e^{.025} - 1) = 2.5\%.$$

We say, then, that each additional year of schooling increases income
by about 10%, while each additional year of age increases income by
about 2.5%.

Another transformation of y that is sometimes useful is the *logit*
transformation, which is applied when y is a *proportion*. Suppose
your sample consists of U.S. cities and y is the proportion of regis-
tered voters who actually voted in the last presidential election. The
logit of y is

$$\log\left(\frac{y}{1-y}\right)$$

For this formula to work, y has to be a number between 0 and 1,
not a percentage. (If your data are in the form of percentages, you

can just change the 1 to 100 in the denominator.) The advantage of the logit transformation is that it preserves both the upper and lower bounds of y. No matter what the values of the independent variables or their coefficients, the predicted value of y will always be a number between 0 and 1.

8.3. What Transformations Are Used for the Independent Variables?

Many different mathematical transformations can be applied to the independent variables in a regression model, but only a few are widely used. Most common are *polynomial* models, which are simply models with integer (whole number) powers of x. For a single explanatory variable x, a *quadratic* polynomial is

$$y = A + B_1 x + B_2 x^2.$$

A *cubic* model is

$$y = A + B_1 x + B_2 x^2 + B_3 x^3.$$

We could keep on adding more powers of x, but you rarely see models that go beyond the third power. Note that whenever you add a higher power, you must always include terms for all the lower-order powers. Of course, other variables could be included in the model as well, but I'll consider only a single x to keep things simple.

Why are polynomial models so popular? One reason is that they can be used with any kind of quantitative variable, whereas most other transformations require that x be measured at the ratio level, as I'll explain later. Another reason is that polynomials can approximate a wide variety of different relationships between x and y. Figure 8.1 shows the basic shape of a quadratic function in which y depends on both x and x^2. The most characteristic feature of this curve is that as x increases, y first increases, then reaches a maximum, and then decreases. If we change the sign of the coefficient for x^2 (from negative to positive), we can flip the curve over so that y decreases until it reaches a minimum, then increases.

A quadratic curve might be a reasonable approximation for the relationship between age and income, where we expect that income first increases with age and then decreases. But what about education and income, where the function should be always increasing? Even in those cases, the quadratic function may be a substantial

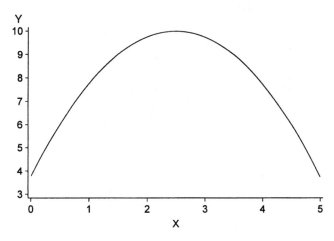

Figure 8.1. Plot of *y* as a Quadratic Function of *x*

improvement over a linear function. For example, Figure 8.2 shows a linear approximation to the logarithmic function. To produce this graph, I generated 500 values of *x* between .01 and 5.0. Then I computed $y = \log x$. Finally, I did a least squares regression of *y* on *x*. Although it's better than nothing, the straight line deviates substantially from the logarithmic curve, especially when *x* is near 0. The R^2 for the linear regression was only .77.

Figure 8.3 shows what happens when you fit a *quadratic* equation (by least squares) to the logarithmic function. Even though the quadratic curve starts to decline at the right-hand side of the curve

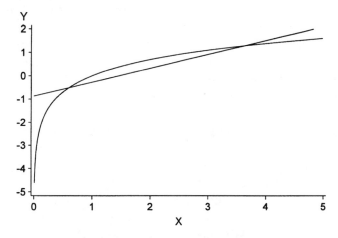

Figure 8.2. A Linear Approximation to a Logarithmic Function

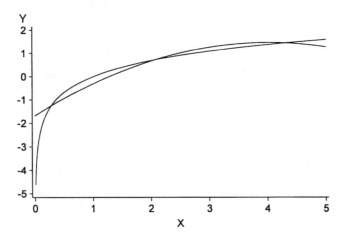

Figure 8.3. A Quadratic Approximation to a Logarithmic Function

while the logarithmic function keeps increasing, we still do much better than the linear function: The R^2 here is .91.

The fit is even better when we fit a cubic function (which has x^3 in the equation), as shown in Figure 8.4. For this approximation the R^2 was .95. We could keep adding more powers of x to get an ever-closer approximation, but the result would be a complicated, unwieldy model. For most social science data, a lower order polynomial is close enough.

Why use a polynomial at all when we could use the logarithmic transformation directly? One reason is that we usually don't know in advance what the true function is. The nice thing about the quadratic function is that, unlike the logarithmic function, it can approximate a wide variety of different curves. It can handle increasing functions, decreasing functions, or functions that reverse direction. Furthermore, the rate of change can be either increasing or decreasing. For even more flexibility, you can use the cubic function.

The other reason why polynomials are attractive is they can be used with *interval level* variables, whereas most other functions require *ratio* level variables. What distinguishes ratio variables is that they have a fixed zero point that is an intrinsic feature of the phenomenon being measured. Good examples of ratio variables are income, number of persons in an organization, or number of hours spent watching TV. With interval variables, on the other hand, the

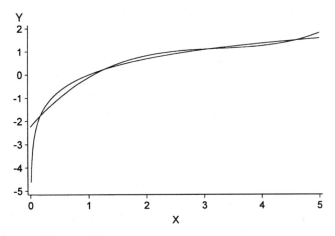

Figure 8.4. A Cubic Approximation to a Logarithmic Function

zero point is completely arbitrary. You can freely change the zero point by adding a constant to everyone's score without losing any information. Most indexes and scales that are constructed by averaging or summing people's responses to questions would have to be considered interval variables, at best. Perhaps the most familiar examples of true interval scales are the Fahrenheit and Celsius scales for measuring temperature. Both scales have (different) zero points that were determined by convention.

Why is the zero point an issue? Many mathematical functions change dramatically when the zero point of the variable changes. These include such common functions as the logarithm of x, the square root of x, and the reciprocal of x. For example, $\log(x + 5)$ will produce a rather different curve from $\log x$. If you use these transformations in a multiple regression, you'll get different coefficients and a different R^2, depending on what constant is added to the variable. Because the zero point on an interval scale is arbitrary, that means that the regression results are arbitrary too. By contrast, polynomial regression functions are invariant to the addition of a constant to everyone's score. The coefficients of the lower-order terms may change, but the R^2, the coefficient for the highest order term, and the coefficients for any other variables will remain the same. Unless you're dealing with a ratio scale, then, you should stick to polynomial transformations or the dummy variable method described in Section 8.5.

8.4. How Can I Check for Nonlinearity?

Suppose you've estimated a linear regression equation and found statistically significant effects for some of the variables. You may then wonder if any of these effects is better described by something other than a strictly linear equation. How can you tell? Scatterplots can be useful if the correlations are high, but for most data in the social sciences they're not much help. The data points are typically so scattered that it's hard enough to see a relationship at all, let alone decide whether it's a straight line or a curve.

Consider the relationship between age and income that we examined in Chapter 5. The scatterplot in Figure 5.1 gave a clear indication that income increases with age, but it also looked as though there might be some decline at older ages. How to tell? Before answering that question, let's first consider a better way to do the plot. Figure 5.1 could be misleading because it ignores the influence of years of schooling. What we really want is a plot of income and age, *controlling* for years of schooling. Such a plot is called a partial residual plot, and some regression programs (e.g., SPSS and SAS) can produce them on request. If you don't have such a program, the plots are not very difficult to construct. For this example, we first regress income on schooling and output the *residuals* (prediction errors) from that regression. Then we regress age on schooling and output the residuals from that regression. Finally, we plot the residuals from the first regression against the residuals from the second regression. The result, produced by SPSS and shown in Figure 8.5, looks a little more linear than Figure 5.1, but it's hard to tell just from a visual examination.

If plots won't do the job, what will? The method I find most useful is to fit a quadratic function to the data. As we've seen, the quadratic is a simple function that can approximate a wide range of different functions. I fit a quadratic function of age to the income data and got the following results:

$$\text{Income} = -69{,}470 + 1{,}454 \text{ Schooling} + 3{,}196 \text{ Age} - 29.54 \text{ Age}^2 \quad R^2 = .31$$
$$(p = .013) \qquad (p = .097) \quad (p = .037)$$

What's most important for our purposes is that the age-squared coefficient is significant. That immediately tells us that there is evidence for nonlinearity. If age-squared had *not* been significant, then we'd say that there is insufficient evidence for anything besides a

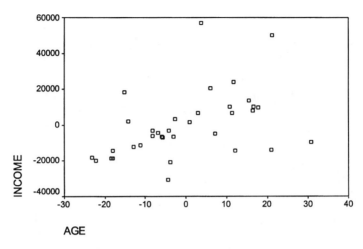

Figure 8.5. Partial Residual Plot of Income on Age

linear relationship. In that case, the next step would be to delete age-squared from the model and go back to a strictly linear model.

So now we know that the relationship is nonlinear, but what sort of nonlinearity is it? Just because we fit a quadratic function doesn't mean it's really quadratic. The quadratic function should be viewed as merely an approximation to the true function, whatever it is. We may never know what that true function is, however, so it makes sense to see what the quadratic function tells us about the relationship between age and income. Although it's possible to draw some conclusions based on the signs and values of the coefficients, the most reliable and complete method is to graph the estimated regression equation. When I graphed the estimated equation above, with Schooling set to its mean value of 12.6, I got the curve in Figure 8.6. This curve tells us that between ages 20 and 54, income rises with age but at a decreasing rate. After 44, income declines with age, at an increasing rate.

It would be a mistake to make too much of the details of this curve, however. We can't be sure that the quadratic function is correct and, even if it were, random variability in the data could produce substantial discrepancies between the graphed curve and the true curve.

At this point, it might be worthwhile to see if we can do any better than the quadratic function. For example, we can fit a cubic

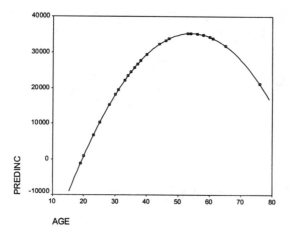

Figure 8.6. Plot of Estimated Regression Line of Income on Age

equation by adding age cubed to the model. When I tried that, I got a p value for the age cubed coefficient of .24, which is not statistically significant, so I deleted the age-cubed variable and went back to the quadratic equation. Because age is a ratio level variable, we might also want to try other kinds of functions, like the logarithm or square root. As it turned out, both of those functions did better than a strictly linear function, but neither did as well as the quadratic (as evaluated by the R^2).

8.5. How Can Dummy Variables Help With Nonlinearity?

To this point, we have been representing nonlinear relationships by way of smooth curves that could be expressed in simple mathematical form. Now we consider an alternative approach to nonlinearity that doesn't make such stringent assumptions about the nature of the relationship.

In Chapter 2, we saw several examples where dichotomous independent variables, like gender or urban/rural, were coded as dummy variables having values of 0 or 1. I explained that the coefficients for such variables could be interpreted as "adjusted" differences in the means of the dependent variable for the two groups. For instance, if the dependent variable is income and the independent variable is a dummy variable for sex, then the estimated coefficient for the dummy variable represents the difference between the average incomes for men and women. If other independent variables are added to the equation, then the coefficient for sex is an average difference that "controls" for the additional variables.

We also saw that dummy variables could be used for nominal (categorical) variables with more than two categories. Here's a quick review. In a typical survey, marital status might have four categories: currently married, never married, divorced, or widowed. To include marital status as an independent variable in a regression model, we would create *three* dummy variables (always one fewer dummy variables than the number of categories). For example,

Never married?   1 = Yes, 0 = No.
Divorced?   1 = Yes, 0 = No.
Widowed?   1 = Yes, 0 = No.

Suppose the dependent variable is the number of hours per week spent on housework. If we regress housework on the three dummy variables, we might get the following regression coefficients:

1.2   Never married
–.5   Divorced
.75   Widowed
8.4   Intercept

Each of the three coefficients is a comparison with the omitted category (reference category), which is currently married. We see that those who have never married spend an average of 1.2 *more* hours per week on housework than the currently married, divorced people spend an average of one-half hour *less* than the currently married, and widowed people spend an average of .75 hours more than the currently married. The intercept, 8.4, is the average number of hours spent on housework by people who are currently married, the reference category. Along with each of the coefficients, there is a *t* statistic and a *p* value. As usual, these test whether the coefficients are significantly different from 0. That means that each *p* value tells us whether there is a significant difference between the average hours spent on housework by people in that category and by people in the reference category, the currently married. Again, if we put other variables in the regression equation, the coefficients for the dummy variables can be interpreted as "adjusted" differences in the means of the dependent variables for the different categories.

It makes no fundamental difference which category is chosen to be the reference (omitted) category. There is some benefit, however, in choosing a reference category that has a relatively large number of people. Suppose, for example, that our reference category was widowed instead of currently married, and there were only 10 widowed people in the sample. Because the number of widowed people is so small, the estimate of the mean hours of housework for this group would be very unreliable—it would have a large standard error. It follows that any comparisons with this group—such as the coefficients for the other categories—would also be very unreliable. As a result, the regression output might tell you that *none* of the other categories is significantly different from the widowed group. There could, however, still be large and highly significant differences between the currently married and the never married, differences that wouldn't show up in the standard output.

Some regression programs allow you to do a "global test" of the hypothesis that all the coefficients for all the dummy variables are equal to 0. This is equivalent to testing whether or not there are *any* differences among the categories. Because this test does not depend on which category is chosen as the reference category, it should be used whenever it's available.

Now we're in a position to talk about using dummy variables to represent nonlinear relationships. It's always possible to take a quantitative variable, like age, and break it down into a set of categories. For instance, the data set described in Section 8.4 had 35 persons with ages ranging from 19 to 76 years old. To treat age as a categorical variable, I chose four age intervals: 19-31, 32-39, 40-54, and 55-76. Then, to include the categorical version of age as an independent variable in a regression model, I created three dummy variables:

$AGE2 = 1$ if $32 \leq AGE \leq 39$, otherwise $AGE2 = 0$

$AGE3 = 1$ if $40 \leq AGE \leq 54$, otherwise $AGE3 = 0$

$AGE4 = 1$ if $55 \leq AGE \leq 76$, otherwise $AGE4 = 0$.

The first age category (19-31) is used as the reference category so no dummy variable is needed. I then estimated a multiple regression with income as the dependent variable; the independent variables

TABLE 8.1 Regression of Income (Thousands of Dollars) on Schooling and Age

Variable	Coefficient	Standard Error	p Value
Intercept	–6,407	11,841	
Schooling	1,683	926	.079
Age (32-39)	1,840	8,033	.820
Age (40-54)	22,991	8,160	.008
Age (55-76)	19,096	8,335	.029
R^2	.38		

were the three age dummies and years of schooling. The results are shown in Table 8.1.

We see, first, that the coefficient for years of schooling is not statistically significant (at least not at the .05 level). Nevertheless, our best estimate is that each additional year of schooling is associated with a $1,683 increase income, controlling for age. Each of the age coefficients is a comparison between the average income in that age category and the reference category, 19-31, after adjusting for schooling. Those in the age interval 32-39 make about $1,840 more than those in the youngest interval, but this difference is not statistically significant. Those in the next age category, 40-54, make an estimated $22,991 more than those in the youngest category, a difference which has a p value less than .01. Those in the 55-76 age category also earn significantly more than those in the youngest category, but now the difference is only about $19,096. We have some evidence now for a decline in income at older ages. The estimated decline from the 40-54 category to the 55-76 category is just the difference in the coefficients: $19,096 – $22,991 = –$3,895. (It's possible to test whether this decline is statistically significant—it isn't.)

Compared with the polynomial models in Section 8.3, there are two advantages to the dummy-variable method for representing nonlinearity in a regression equation:

- The method doesn't impose any particular pattern on the relationship between independent and dependent variables
- The numerical results can be somewhat simpler to interpret

As with most statistical methods, however, there are disadvantages as well. For one thing, the division of the variable into intervals is somewhat arbitrary; instead of four age categories, I could have used five categories, with somewhat different results. Another concern is that the dummy-variable method usually estimates more coefficients than, say, a quadratic model. Whenever you estimate more things with the same number of cases, the precision with which you can estimate any one of them goes down. This is especially problematic when the sample is small. So the dummy variable method is most attractive when the sample is on the large side (which it certainly is not for the age-income example).

8.6. What Is Interaction?

There is another kind of nonlinearity—called *interaction*—that involves two or more independent variables rather than just one. In a linear regression model with two independent variables

$$y = A + B_1 x_1 + B_2 x_2 + U$$

the "effect" of each variable is always the same. A one-unit increase in x_1 always produces a change of B_1 units in y. Now we want to consider the possibility that the effect of x_1 may be different under different conditions. Specifically, let's suppose that the effect of x_1 depends on the value of the other variable, x_2. It's easy to imagine situations in which this might happen. We would certainly expect that additional years of schooling might be more financially rewarding for highly intelligent people than for those at the low end of the IQ scale. We also know that income increases more rapidly with age for doctors and lawyers than it does for construction workers and farm laborers. In that case, we say that there is an interaction between age and occupation in their effects on income.

How can we represent this notion of interaction in a regression equation? Continuing with our three-variable example, let's suppose our aim is to write an equation in which the effect of age depends on the level of schooling. Specifically, let's suppose that the slope of income on age is steeper for those with more education. There are many possible ways to represent this idea, but the simplest and most widely used is to assume that the coefficient for age is a linear function of years of schooling. If B_1 is the coefficient for age, and x_2 is years of schooling, we write

$$B_1 = C + D x_2$$

TABLE 8.2 Regression of Income on Schooling, Age, and Their Interaction

Variable	Coefficient	Standard Error	p Value
Intercept	88,159	33,131	
Schooling	–7,649	2,696	.012
Age	–1,770	659	.008
Schooling × Age	207	55.4	.001
R^2	.50		

where C and D are numbers to be estimated. The number C can be interpreted as the effect of age when years of schooling is 0. The coefficient D tells us how much the effect of age changes with each one-unit increase in schooling. Our hypothesis that the age effect is stronger for those with more education implies that D should be a positive number.

How do we estimate such a model? Well, if we substitute the "auxiliary" equation for B_1 into the original three-variable equation, we get

$$y = A + (C + Dx_2)x_1 + B_2x_2.$$

We can then multiply the terms in parentheses by x_1 and rearrange things to get

$$y = A + Cx_1 + B_2x_2 + Dx_2x_1.$$

This equation has both x_1 and x_2 entered in the usual way, but it also has the *product* of x_1 and x_2 as an additional variable. This form of the equation is easily estimated with standard software. Just create a new variable z that is equal to the product of x_1 and x_2, and run a regression of y on x_1, x_2, and z. When I did that for the 35 cases in Table 1.1, I got the results in Table 8.2.

When you estimate a model with an interaction term, the first thing you should look at is the p value for the product of the two variables. In this case, it is less than .001, far below the usual .05 criterion for statistical significance, so we conclude that there is strong evidence in these data that the effect of age depends on the level of schooling. If the product term had not been significant, then a reasonable strategy would be to drop the product term from the model and revert to a model without an interaction.

The coefficients for schooling and age are also statistically significant, but their signs are *negative*, indicating that increases in age

TABLE 8.3

Years of Schooling	Effect of Age on Income
9	93
12	714
14	1,128
16	1,542
20	2,370

and schooling produce decreases in income. How can this be? What you must always remember is that in models with interactions, the main-effect coefficients have a special (and often not very useful) meaning. The coefficient of –1,770 for age in Table 8.2 can be interpreted as the effect of age *when schooling is 0*. Similarly, the coefficient of –7,649 for schooling can be interpreted as the effect of schooling *when age is 0*. Obviously, a value of 0 for age is impossible and a value of 0 for schooling is improbable. In general, whenever you have a product term in a regression model, you should not be concerned about the statistical significance (or lack thereof) of the main effects of the two variables in the product. That doesn't mean that you can delete the main effects from the model. Like the intercept in any regression equation, those terms play an essential role in generating correct predictions for the dependent variable.

How do you interpret a regression model when the product term *is* statistically significant? The way to interpret the coefficients in Table 8.2 is to calculate the effect of age on income for different values of schooling. As we saw earlier, the effect of age on income is a linear function of schooling: $-1{,}770 + (207 \times \text{schooling})$. By choosing some typical schooling values and applying this formula, we can get the estimated effects of age under different conditions, as shown in Table 8.3. This table tells us that the income increases with age more than twice as fast for someone with 16 years of education as compared to someone with 12 years of education.

There's another way to interpret Table 8.2, however. Remember that putting a product term in a regression equation is symmetrical with respect to the two variables. That means that we can also look at how the effect of schooling varies with age. In this case, the effect of schooling is given by $-7{,}649 + (207 \times \text{age})$. Applying this to some possible values of age, we get the results in Table 8.4. This tells us that the effect of schooling on income changes dramatically with age. For those age 35, each additional year of schooling yields a

TABLE 8.4

Age	Effect of Schooling on Income
25	–2,474
35	–404
45	1,666
55	3,736
65	5,806

decrease of $404 of income, but among those age 55, each additional year of schooling yields an additional $3,736 in income.

Why should schooling have a negative effect on income at earlier ages? One possible explanation is that at age 25, people who didn't go to college already have had several years of employment experience, whereas those who did go to college are just entering the labor market. With increasing age, however, college-educated persons experience substantial increases in income while those without a college education have incomes that are relatively flat.

8.7. How Do I Interpret Interactions With Dummy Variables?

Dummy variables can be included in product terms just like any other variable, but if one of the variables in an interaction is a dummy variable, the results have a special interpretation that we'll examine briefly. Consider the results in Table 8.5 for our sample of 35 men. This table shows the regression of income on years of schooling, age, a dummy for marital status (married = 1, unmarried = 0), and the product of these two variables.

The product term is statistically significant, so we may conclude that there is an interaction between marital status and years of schooling. This means that the effect of schooling depends on marital status and the effect of marital status depends on schooling. But we can be more specific. The main effect of schooling (–$980) is the effect of schooling when marital status is 0, that is, when the person is unmarried. So among those who are not married, each additional year of schooling produces a *decrease* of $980 in income (on average). This number, however, is not statistically different from 0.

TABLE 8.5 Regression of Income (Dollars) on Schooling, Marital Status, and Their Interaction

Variable	Coefficient	p Value
Age	652	.003
Schooling	−980	.57
Married	−48,592	.04
Schooling × Married	3,912	.04
Intercept	8,404	

The coefficient for the product term ($3,912) is the *additional* effect of schooling when the person is married, so the effect of schooling for married respondents is −980 + 3,912 = 2,932: Each additional year of schooling brings $2,932 more income. These relationships are graphed in Figure 8.7, which shows one regression line for married respondents and another for unmarried respondents. If we had fit a model *without* a product term, the slopes for married and unmarried would be equal, and the two lines would be strictly parallel.

We can also interpret the interaction with respect to how the effect of marital status varies with schooling. The coefficient for married (−$48,592) says that among men with no education, those who are married make about $49,000 less than those who are unmarried. Because no one in the sample has 0 years of schooling, this difference is an extrapolation that should be interpreted with caution. Among those with 6 years of schooling, the income difference between married and unmarried is −48,592 + 6(3,912) = −25,120. That is, married people with 6 years of schooling make about $25,000 less than unmarried people. Among those with 12 years of schooling, the difference is −48,592 + 12(3,912) = −1,648. At 20 years of schooling, the difference is −48,592 + 20(3,912) = +26,648. All these numbers correspond graphically to the differences between the two lines in Figure 8.7 at each level of schooling.

Chapter Highlights

1. The linear regression model is linear in the coefficients but not necessarily linear in the variables. That means that the model will

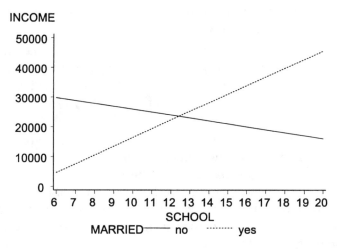

Figure 8.7. Regression of Income on Schooling by Marital Status

accommodate any mathematical transformations of the variables without difficulty. We may want to transform variables to make the model correspond to some theory or fit the data better.

2. Some transformations of the dependent variable can reduce heteroscedasticity, but they also fundamentally change the relationship between the dependent and independent variables in ways that make it hard to interpret the results.

3. For dependent variables that are always greater than 0, the logarithmic transformation can be useful. It ensures that predicted values are always positive, and it allows the coefficients to be interpreted in terms of percentage changes.

4. The logit transformation is useful for dependent variables that are proportions or percentages.

5. Polynomial functions are the most popular transformations of the independent variables. They can be used with any kind of quantitative variable, and they can approximate a wide variety of different shapes.

6. Polynomials are constructed by putting integer powers of x in the regression model. If x^n is in the model, then the model should also include $x^{n-1}, x^{n-2}, \ldots$, and x.

7. The most common polynomial function is the quadratic, which has both x and x^2 in the regression model. Although the resulting

curve has a reversal of direction, it can be used to approximate curves that have no reversal.

8. The easiest way to test for nonlinearity for a particular variable x is to fit a quadratic function by including x^2 in the model. If the coefficient for x^2 is significantly different from 0, that is evidence for nonlinearity. If it's not significant, then you might as well stick to a strictly linear model.

9. When creating dummy variables to represent a categorical variable with more than two categories, the model does not depend on which category is chosen to be the omitted category. It's usually desirable, however, to choose an omitted category with a fairly large number of cases. If the omitted category has a small number of cases, the coefficients for the included categories will have large standard errors.

10. When representing a categorical variable by a set of dummy variables, it's desirable to perform a global test of whether all the dummies have coefficients of 0. This test does not depend on which category is chosen as the omitted category.

11. You can allow for a nonlinear effect of a quantitative variable by creating a set of dummy variables corresponding to different intervals on the quantitative scale.

12. The standard linear model says that the effect of each variable on the dependent variable is always the same, regardless of the values of other variables. Sometimes, however, we want models that embody the idea of interaction—that the effect of one variable may depend on the values of other variables.

13. The most common way to represent interaction in a regression model is to add a new variable that is the product of two variables already in the model. Such models implicitly say that the slope for each of the two variables is a linear function of the other variable.

14. In models with a product term, the main-effect coefficients represent the effect of that variable when the other variable has a value of 0.

15. The best way to interpret a regression model with a product term is to calculate the effects of each of the two variables for a range of different values on the other variable.

16. When one of the variables in a product term is a dummy variable, the model can be interpreted by splitting up the regression into two separate regressions, one for each of the two values of the dummy variable.

Questions to Think About

1. Suppose you transform each of the independent variables in a regression model by subtracting its mean and dividing by its standard deviation. How will the R^2 in the transformed model compare with the R^2 in the model for the original, untransformed variables?

2. In a study of juvenile delinquency, the dependent variable is the number of arrests in a 2-year period, and the independent variables include parental income, parental education, and measures of school performance. Because there is considerable heteroscedasticity, a colleague suggests taking the square root of the dependent variable. Is this a good idea? Why or why not?

3. For a sample of employed women, the dependent variable in a regression analysis is the logarithm of the number of hours per week spent on housework. One of the independent variables is a dummy variable for employed (0) or not employed (1). It has a coefficient of .50. How can this be interpreted?

4. What's wrong with the following regression model?

$$\hat{y} = b_0 + b_1 x + b_2 z^2 + b_3 z^3$$

5. Suppose you estimate a regression model that includes both age and age squared as independent variables. The p values for both age and age-squared are above .40. Is it reasonable to conclude that age has no effect on the dependent variable?

6. For a sample of 200 people, the dependent variable in a multiple regression is amount of money contributed last year to political candidates. The model includes a set of three dummy variables representing party affiliation: one for Democrat, one for Republican, and one for Independent. The omitted category includes all people who do not fit in one of these three categories (e.g., Socialist

Workers Party, Libertarian Party, etc.). None of the three dummies has a statistically significant coefficient. Is it reasonable to conclude that political affiliation doesn't affect contributions? Is there a better way to set up the dummy variables?

7. For a sample of 474 employees, current salary was regressed on

   Minority Classification: 1 = minority, 0 = nonminority

   Educational Level: years of schooling

   EDMIN: Minority Classification × Years of Schooling

Box 8.1 shows the results of the regression, as reported by SPSS. How would you interpret these results?

BOX 8.1. Coefficients[a]

Model	Unstandardized Coefficients		Standardized Coefficients		
	B	Std. Error	Beta	t	Sig.
1 (Constant)	−23028.8	3077.537		−7.483	.000
Minority Classification	31477.287	6953.429	.764	4.527	.000
Educational Level (years)	4312.077	219.726	.729	19.625	.000
EDMIN	−2725.021	526.904	−.865	−5.172	.000

a. Dependent variable: Current salary

9 How Is Multiple Regression Related to Other Statistical Techniques?

Multiple regression is closely related to many other statistical methods that are in common use today. In fact, several methods are exactly equivalent to multiple regression but go by different names. Other methods involve extensions of multiple regression to more complicated situations. Finally, there are several classes of nonlinear models that have the same general aim as multiple regression but make allowance for special features of the dependent variable. The goal of this chapter is to give you a quick overview of these methods and to explain how they are related to multiple regression. Obviously, I can't provide enough information here to enable you to actually use any of these methods.

9.1. How Is Regression Related to Correlation?

I already answered this question in Chapter 5, but a brief review may be helpful here. Both regression and correlation assume that the relationship between the dependent and independent variables can be described by a straight line. Regression focuses on the slope of the line, whereas correlation focuses on the degree to which the data points are scattered around the line. In the bivariate case, testing whether the regression slope is equal to zero is equivalent to testing whether the correlation is equal to zero. When there are multiple independent variables, testing whether a regression slope is zero is equivalent to testing whether the corresponding *partial* correlation is zero. Finally, the R^2 for a regression is equal to the squared correlation between the dependent variable and the predicted value of the dependent variable, based on the estimated regression model.

9.2. How Is Regression Related to the *t* Test for a Difference Between Means?

Suppose you have a sample with both men and women, and you want to test whether the average income for men is greater than the average income for women. The conventional way of doing this is to compute a *t* statistic for the difference between the means (using a pooled variance estimate). Alternatively, you could do a regression of income on a dummy variable for sex. The *t* statistic for the coefficient of this dummy variable will be *identical* to that for the conventional *t* test. The advantage of doing it with regression is that you can control for other variables by putting them in the equation.

9.3. What Is Analysis of Variance?

Analysis of variance (ANOVA) is a method that is widely used to analyze data from experiments with complex treatment designs (Iversen & Norpoth, 1987). In its simplest form, one-way ANOVA is used to test whether the means of the outcome variable are different across two or more groups. When there are only two groups, ANOVA is equivalent to a conventional *t* test for a difference in means and, therefore, it's also equivalent to a multiple regression with a single, independent dummy variable. When there are more than two groups, one-way ANOVA is exactly equivalent to a multiple regression with dummy variables for all but one of the groups. Even for multifactor designs, there is virtually always a multiple regression model that is exactly equivalent to the ANOVA model. Many statistical packages don't even have separate ANOVA and multiple regression programs anymore. Instead, they have a single procedure that estimates the so-called *general linear model*.

9.4. What Is Analysis of Covariance?

Analysis of covariance (ANCOVA) is an extension of ANOVA to allow for situations where some of the independent variables are categorical (as with experimental treatments) and some are measured on quantitative scales, often called covariates (Wildt & Ahtola,

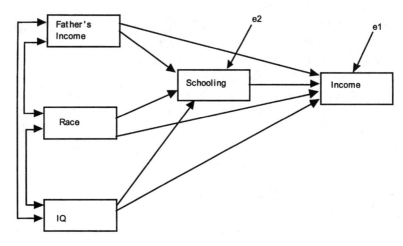

Figure 9.1. Path Diagram for Regressions of Income and Schooling

1978). Of course, we already know how to do that with multiple regression: Just put the quantitative variables in the regression and include a set of dummy variables to represent each of the categorical variables. As you might expect from the last two questions, the multiple regression model is exactly equivalent to the corresponding ANCOVA model.

9.5. What Is Path Analysis?

Path analysis is a technique that became extremely popular in sociology in the late 1960s and then spread to other social sciences (Duncan, 1975). Essentially, it is a way of representing a set of regression equations with "causal" diagrams. Its popularity stemmed from the fact that the diagrams made it easy to understand a complex set of relationships that might otherwise be obscure if you looked only at the equations.

Figure 9.1 shows a path diagram for the dependence of income and schooling on father's income, race, and IQ. This diagram corresponds to two regression equations:

Schooling = a_0 + a_1Race + a_2IQ + a_3Father's Income + e_2

Income = b_0 + b_1Schooling + b_2Race + b_3IQ + b_4Father's Income + e_1.

In a path analysis, the *a* and *b* coefficients can be estimated separately for each equation by ordinary least squares.

In the diagram, each of the single-headed arrows represents a causal effect of one variable on another. The double-headed arrows represent correlations that don't involve any presumption of causality. It is common (but not essential) to put numbers on the single-headed arrows. Usually these are standardized regression coefficients, but they may also be unstandardized coefficients.

Although path analysis doesn't really involve anything new with regard to statistical estimation, it can be very helpful in the analysis of direct and indirect effects, an issue that we discussed in Chapter 3. In particular, path analysis has some easy to use rules for calculating indirect effects by tracing along pathways in the diagrams.

9.6. What Are Simultaneous Equation Models?

The path model that we just examined is an example of a more general class of linear models called simultaneous equation models. The essence of such models is that there is more than one equation, and all equations are simultaneously true.

Recursive simultaneous equation models, like the one in Figure 9.1, can be estimated by ordinary least squares applied to each equation separately. A model is recursive if the causal relationships flow in only one direction. In terms of path diagrams, that means that if you follow the single-headed arrows, you can't get back to where you started from.

Figure 9.2 shows a simple *non*recursive system. In this model, occupational aspirations affect educational aspirations but, at the same time, educational aspirations affect occupational aspirations. The two equations in this model *must* be estimated simultaneously, and ordinary least squares will not do the job. The best known methods for estimating nonrecursive models are two-stage least squares, three-stage least squares, and maximum likelihood, but there are many others. Unfortunately, the validity of any of these methods rests on assumptions that may be difficult to justify. For the model in Figure 9.2, for example, it is necessary to assume that father's income does *not* directly affect educational aspirations, and that father's education does *not* directly affect occupational aspirations.

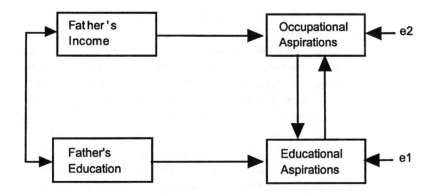

Figure 9.2. Path Diagram of a Nonrecursive Model

9.7. What Is Factor Analysis?

Factor analysis is designed to take a bunch of variables and reduce them to a much smaller number of dimensions (Kim & Mueller, 1978a, 1978b). Suppose, for example, that you have an interview schedule that contains 40 questions about attitudes toward illegal drugs. If you did a factor analysis of these questions, you might find that the responses to these questions could be accounted for by three underlying dimensions: parental concern, liberal versus conservative, and fear of crime. For each observed variable, you would get an estimate of how strongly it depends on one or more of these underlying dimensions.

The model that forms the basis of factor analysis is a linear, simultaneous equations model. Each observed variable is the dependent variable in a single equation. The independent variables are all latent, unobserved variables called *factors*. For four observed variables (y_1 through y_4) and a single factor F, the factor model can be written as

$$y_1 = a_1 F + e_1$$

$$y_2 = a_2 F + e_2$$

$$y_3 = a_3 F + e_3$$

$$y_4 = a_4 F + e_4$$

The as are like ordinary regression coefficients, but they are commonly referred to as *factor loadings*. Like all factor models, this one says that whatever correlations we find among the *y*s can be completely explained by their mutual dependence on *F*.

Because the independent variables in the linear equations are not directly measured, ordinary least squares cannot be used to estimate the factor loadings. Many different methods are available, but they generally fall into two classes, *exploratory factor analysis* and *confirmatory factor analysis*. In confirmatory factor analysis, the analyst must specify exactly how many factors there are in the model, and which observed variables depend on which factors. In exploratory factor analysis, these decisions are left to the computer algorithm. Although that may seem like a big advantage, the problem with exploratory factor analysis is that different algorithms may come up with very different results. Nowadays, confirmatory factor analysis is generally preferred, at least in those situations where you can make some reasonable guesses about what the model should look like.

9.8. What Are Structural Equation Models?

Structural equation models combine confirmatory factor analysis with simultaneous equations models (Bollen, 1989; Hayduk, 1988). The basic idea is that the observed variables depend on latent, unobserved variables, and those latent variables may have causal relationships among them. Because the models are often rather complicated, they are frequently presented in the form of path diagrams. Figure 9.3 is a path diagram showing how a son's socioeconomic status (SES) depends on his father's SES and his mother's SES. The three SES variables are all latent variables. Each has two observed indicators: occupational prestige and years of schooling. The diagram follows the usual convention that all the observed variables are rectangles and all the unobserved variables are ovals; it is incomplete because I have omitted the error terms for all the dependent variables.

When this model is written in the form of equations (five of them), each equation looks like an ordinary regression equation. But again, because some of the variables are not directly observed, specialized software is needed to estimate the model. The best-known programs are LISREL (Jöreskog, 1997), EQS (Byrne, 1994), and Amos (Arbuckle, 1998).

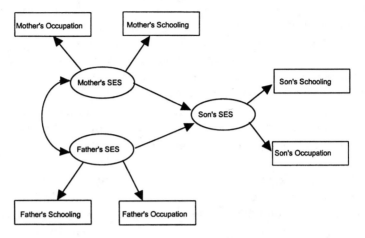

Figure 9.3. Path Diagram of a Structural Equation Model

Why would anyone want to estimate a model like this? There are two reasons. First, these methods can correct for the biasing effect of measurement error that I discussed in Chapter 3. Second, the methods can be helpful in dealing with multicollinearity (Chapter 7) that often occurs when you have several independent variables that may be measuring the same thing.

9.9. What Are Multilevel Models?

Multilevel models, also known as *hierarchical linear models*, are designed for data in which the observations are naturally clustered into groups (Bryk & Raudenbush, 1992; Kreft & De Leeuw, 1998). Imagine a survey of fourth-grade students in which the first step is to take a sample of *classrooms* from around the country. Then within each classroom, 10 students are chosen to be in the study, so students are clustered within classrooms. Suppose that the dependent variable y is a score on an academic achievement test, and the independent variable x is a measure of the child's IQ. (I'll stick with a single independent variable to keep things simple.)

Ignoring the classrooms, we could use ordinary least squares to estimate a bivariate regression model for the entire sample of the form

$$y = A + Bx + U,$$

where U is a random disturbance term. Although this would not be completely wrong (the coefficients should be unbiased), it's likely that this regression would violate the "uncorrelated disturbances" assumption discussed in Chapter 6. Specifically, we would expect the U variables for students in the same classroom to be correlated. That's because, for a variety of reasons, students in the same classroom tend to be more alike in academic performance than students in different classrooms. The consequences of violating this assumption are standard errors that are too low and test statistics that are too high.

One way to solve this problem is to estimate a multilevel model that takes the classroom structure into account. To do this, let's put some subscripts on the variables, with i denoting the student and j denoting the classroom:

$$y_{ij} = A_j + B_j x_{ij} + U_{ij}.$$

This is the student-level equation. Notice that besides putting subscripts on the variables, I've also put a j subscript on the intercept and the slope. This allows for the possibility that the slope and intercept may vary from one classroom to another. But how?

Let's suppose we've also measured the variable z_j, which is the number of years of experience of the teacher in each classroom. We can now write a classroom-level equation in which the slope and intercept at the student level depend on the teacher's experience:

$$A_j = C + Dz_j + E_j$$

$$B_j = F + Gz_j + H_j.$$

If we had several classrooms within each school, we could have additional school-level equations in which the intercepts and coefficients at the classroom level depend on variables measured at the school level.

Besides producing correct standard errors, the appeal of the multilevel model lies in its capacity to reveal how processes at the individual level are affected by things going on at the group level. As with many of the more advanced methods we've looked at in this chapter, the estimation of multilevel models requires specialized software. There are well-known standalone packages like HLM and MLn, but some of the more comprehensive packages like SAS and Stata can also estimate these models.

9.10. What Is Nonlinear Regression?

In Chapter 8, we saw how different kinds of nonlinear models could be estimated with ordinary least squares by performing transformations on the variables before doing the analysis. Some nonlinear models cannot be estimated in this way, however. Suppose, for example, that you think the relationship between x and y can best be described by the equation

$$y = 1 + Ax^B$$

where A and B are constants to be estimated. In this case, there's no way to transform the variables so that the equation can be estimated by ordinary least squares.

You may be asking yourself, "Why would I ever want to estimate an equation like this?" In sociology or political science, that's a hard question to answer, but economists do this sort of thing all the time. They construct mathematical theories of economic relationships, from which they derive testable equations that are often too nonlinear for ordinary least squares. So how do they do it? There are a variety of different techniques for estimating nonlinear regression models, but the best known is nonlinear least squares (Seber & Wild, 1989).

The basic principle of nonlinear least squares is exactly the same as ordinary least squares: Choose values of the parameters that minimize the sum of the squared prediction errors. Unfortunately, in the nonlinear case there's usually no explicit formula that produces parameter estimates that satisfy the least squares criterion. Instead, it's necessary to use an *iterative algorithm*, which can be described as a process of successive approximations. You start with reasonable guesses of the unknown parameters, called *starting values*. You plug the starting values into a formula that produces another set of numbers that are, you hope, closer to the correct solution. Then you take those numbers and plug them into the same formula to produce a third set of estimates. The process continues in this way until there's virtually no change from one *iteration* to the next. Then we say that the algorithm has converged. Of course, the computer handles all the details of this process. Many statistical packages have procedures that perform nonlinear least squares, or some similar estimation technique.

9.11. What Is Logit Analysis?

Logit analysis—also known as *logistic regression* analysis—is a very popular regression method for *dichotomous dependent variables* (Long, 1997; Menard, 1995). Suppose, for example, that you want to estimate a regression model for explaining why some students attend college while others do not. For a sample of 19-year-olds, you could create a dummy variable with a value of 1 if they were enrolled in college, and a value of 0 if they were not enrolled. Then you could estimate a linear regression of this variable on explanatory variables like high school GPA, family income, and parents' education.

Although this isn't such a bad method—it was widely used 20 years ago—most researchers now consider it unacceptable. The problem is that dummy dependent variables necessarily violate two assumptions of the linear regression model: homoscedasticity and normality of the disturbance. The details aren't worth our attention here. Alternative methods that don't suffer from these problems include logit analysis, probit analysis, and complementary log-log analysis. The most popular by far is logit analysis. Here's a brief explanation.

Let p be the probability that a student is enrolled in college. If we have two independent variables, x_1 and x_2, the logit model says that

$$\log\left(\frac{p}{1-p}\right) = A + B_1 x_1 + B_2 x_2.$$

The expression on the left-hand side of this equation is called the *logit* of p. The purpose of this transformation is to convert a variable that is bounded by 0 and 1 into a variable that has no upper or lower bounds.

The most widely used method for estimating the logit model is something called *maximum likelihood*. Like nonlinear regression, maximum likelihood usually requires an iterative algorithm to produce the estimates. Although logit analysis has many things going for it, the coefficients can be more difficult to interpret than ordinary regression coefficients.

9.12. What Is Event History Analysis?

Event history analysis is a regression method that is used for explaining or predicting the *timing of events* (Allison, 1984, 1995). The method was first developed by biostatisticians who called it *survival analysis* because they wanted to model the survival times of cancer patients. It turns out that the same methodology can be used for all sorts of events in the social sciences: births, marriages, divorces, job changes, residence changes, promotions, school dropouts, arrests, and so on. In fact, it's remarkable just how many of the things that social scientists study can be treated as events.

Why do we need a special methodology for events? For two reasons: *censoring* and *time dependent explanatory variables*. Suppose you want to develop a regression model to explain why some marriages last longer than others. You get a sample of couples who were married in, say, 1990, and you follow them for 10 years to see how long the marriages last. Let y be length of each marriage, in months. You want to estimate a regression of y on such variables as wife's age at marriage, husband's age at marriage, wife's education, and husband's education. There's a problem: Two-thirds of the marriages were still intact at the end of 10 years. The marriages that are still in progress when the study ends are called *censored*. You could delete the censored cases from the analysis, but that's losing an awful lot of data. Or you could set the marriage length at 120 months, but that's clearly an underestimate.

Before we discuss solutions to the censoring problem, there's another problem to consider: time dependent explanatory variables. Suppose you want to include number of children as one of the explanatory variables. This seems like a natural thing to do, but the number of children changes over time. You wouldn't want to count the number of children only at the end of the marriage because that would produce an artifactual positive relationship. On average, if a marriage lasts longer, there's more time available to have children.

The most popular method for dealing with both these problems is something called Cox regression, named after its inventor, Sir David Cox (1972). Cox regression has two components: a model known as the *proportional hazards model* and an estimation method called *partial likelihood*. The proportional hazards model (for two explanatory variables) can be written as

$$\log h(t) = A + B_1 x_1 + B_2 x_2.$$

In this equation, $h(t)$ is the *instantaneous likelihood* of an event at time t. Partial likelihood is an iterative estimation method that is very similar to the maximum likelihood method used in logit analysis.

There are many other methods of event history analysis, including Kaplan-Meier estimation of survival curves, log-rank tests for differences in survival curves, accelerated failure time models, and discrete-time logit models. All these methods solve the problem of censoring, but not all deal with time-dependent explanatory variables.

Chapter Highlights

1. Correlation is intimately related to regression. The correlation coefficient merely describes the degree of scatter around a regression line.

2. The usual t test for a difference between two means is equivalent to regressing the variable of interest y on a dummy variable that distinguishes the two groups.

3. Analysis of variance is equivalent to multiple regression in which the independent variables are dummy variables representing different categories.

4. Analysis of covariance is equivalent to multiple regression in which some of the independent variables are dummy variables and some are interval level variables.

5. Path analysis is a method for representing a set of regression equations by way of diagrams. It is helpful in understanding and analyzing direct and indirect effects.

6. Simultaneous equations models are used to represent *reciprocal* (two-way) relationships among variables. The estimation of such models requires special techniques and somewhat demanding assumptions.

7. Factor analysis is a method for taking a set of variables and reducing them to a smaller number of dimensions. It assumes

that the observed variables are linear functions of a set of unob-served or latent variables.

8. Structural equations models combine confirmatory factor analy-sis with simultaneous equation models.

9. Multilevel models are linear models designed for situations in which units at one level (e.g., persons) are clustered into larger units (e.g., schools). They can help us understand how individual behavior is affected by group characteristics.

10. Nonlinear regression analysis is a set of methods for estimating nonlinear equations that are too complicated to be handled by ordinary least squares.

11. Logit analysis is the most popular method for regression analysis when the dependent variable is a dichotomy. It avoids the viola-tions of assumptions that occur when you do OLS regression with a dummy dependent variable.

12. Event history analysis is a regression method for predicting the timing of events. It is designed to solve two problems: censoring and time dependent explanatory variables.

Answers to Questions to Think About

Chapter 1

1. At most 12 variables can be entered because the number of independent variables must be less than the number of cases. In practice, you would want far fewer than 12 independent variables.

2. The slope is more important because it tells how one variable changes when the other variable changes.

3. It would be natural to choose television time as the dependent variable and age as the independent variable. We know that time spent watching television cannot affect a person's age. I would expect a nonlinear relationship, with television time decreasing with age until sometime in middle age, then increasing with age.

4. As the percentage foreign born increases by one percentage point, the percentage of people unemployed increases by .20 points.

5. An R^2 of .15 is rather low for a prediction equation. It would be rather risky to use this as a major factor in determining college admission.

6. He has not proven that being overweight causes depression. For one thing, the association between body mass and depression could easily be explained by depression causing overeating and, hence, excess body mass.

Chapter 2

1. The original difference of $17,000 between salaries of men and women is "explained away" by differences in work experience. In other words, salary is largely determined by work experience, and men happen to have more.

2. Because age and gender are measured in completely different units, the coefficients for these variables cannot be compared legitimately. On the other hand, he can conclude that the difference in happiness between men and women is larger than the difference between married and unmarried people.

3. For males at birth (age 0), the predicted time spent watching TV is 1.5 hours. This clearly impossible number results from making predictions outside the range of the data.

4. Regression analysis of this ordinal dependent variable presumes that moving from "satisfactory" to "good" is equivalent to moving from "good" to "very good," and so on. This may not be a reasonable assumption.

5. It appears that larger brain size is associated with higher intelligence, even when gender, height, and weight are controlled.

6. Females have lower IQ than males, and IQ goes down with body weight. However, both coefficients are far from statistically significant and could easily be due to random variation alone.

7. If we had only looked at Model 1, we might suspect that the brain size effect was due to differences in body size. Model 2 eliminated that possibility. In fact, the relationship between brain size and IQ gets stronger when we control for other factors.

8. $t = -2.767/1.447 = -1.91$. This statistic has $38 - 5 = 33$ degrees of freedom. Consulting a t table, we find that the p value is between .10 and .05. Using a computer, the exact p value is .065.

9. In Model 1, the constant represents the predicted IQ when brain size equals 0. In Model 2, the constant represents the predicted IQ when all four variables are 0. Because, according to Model 2, IQ goes down with increases in height, the predicted IQ is fairly high when height is 0.

10. You can certainly get better predictions with Model 2, but if the "wrong" variables are in the model, the results for Model 2 could be very misleading.

Chapter 3

1. At the job level, important omitted variables might include prestige of the job, part-time vs. full-time employment, union vs. nonunion, industry category, and size of establishment. At the employee level, omitted variables that might be related to both salary and job satisfaction include tenure in the job, gender, intelligence, physical health, and emotional health.

2. The most plausible rival hypothesis is that depression causes loss of sleep.

3. The causal ordering is ambiguous. There's insufficient basis for choosing one or the other.

4. Because of the time ordering and the likely goal of the study, GPA should be the dependent variable and SAT should be the independent variable.

5. The key weakness is that people may not do a good job of rating their own stress levels. As a result, the statistical control for stress may be inadequate.

6. The sample size may be too small to detect real and substantial differences between those who did and did not take zinc lozenges.

7. Because of the large sample size, the difference between public and private schools may be very small even though it is statistically significant. The magnitude of the coefficient should be evaluated carefully.

8. The statistician has controlled for key intervening variables, potentially obscuring the effect of home versus away. In other words, the home advantage may affect hits, strikeouts, and batting averages, which may, in turn, affect the number of points scored.

9. The problem is that system software may be too highly correlated with machine type to get reliable estimates of their distinct effects.

Chapter 5

1. The predicted income is $32,000. The regression line must cross at the intersection of the two means.

2. $b = .30(8,000)/10 = 240$, and $a = 32,000 - 240(44) = 21,440$.

3. Divorce = –2.489 + .168(Mobility). R^2 = .73. The coefficient is highly significant. It probably is unwise to interpret this as a causal effect because there are too many potential omitted variables, including income and education. In addition, a high rate of divorce might lead to a higher mobility rate.

4. No. They could have the same lines but different degrees of scatter around the lines.

5. If the correlation is statistically significant, the bivariate regression slope will be statistically significant. On the other hand, with regression Jones could control for other variables.

6. You could get an R^2 for the neural network analysis by computing the correlation between the predicted and observed rainfall, then squaring the result.

7. No, the relationship might be nonlinear. There could be an optimal level of advertising, with either too much or too little advertising leading to lower profits.

8. The comprehensive school has more variation in age, which should produce better estimates of the regression coefficient.

9. t = –.753/.310 = –2.43. This is above the critical value of 2.0, so we say that this coefficient is significantly different from 0. Confidence interval: –.753 ± 2(.310) = (–1.373, –.133).

10. All the residuals for x will be 0. Because there's no variation in x^*, you can't estimate the regression of y^* on x^*.

Chapter 6

1. The assumptions of multiple regression tell us under what conditions least squares produces optimal results. The method may still be more useful than other methods even when those assumptions are not met.

2. We want to avoid any systematic tendency to overestimate or underestimate the true value. If we have unbiasedness, we can usually get closer to the true value by taking a bigger sample.

3. The regression coefficients in the sample will be unbiased estimates of the corresponding coefficients in the population.

4. The standard errors tell us how much the regression coefficients are likely to vary from one sample to another. If the sample is

moderate to large in size, 95% of the sample estimates will be within two standard errors of the true coefficients. The smaller the standard errors, the more likely it is that our sample estimate will be close to the true value.

5. If U can have any value, then for any linear equation we choose, there is always some value of U that will make it true.

6. The U term can be thought of as containing all the effects of omitted variables. If some omitted variable is correlated with a measured x variable, then as that x increases, the mean of U will also change.

7. If the regression model contains all the measured variables in the data set, then there's no way to check the mean independence assumption. The assumption could still be violated, however. For example, an important variable may have been omitted (poverty, for instance, could affect juvenile delinquency but might not be in the data set).

8. The estimated coefficients are still unbiased. In most cases, heteroscedasticity doesn't bias the standard errors enough to cause erroneous conclusions. Still, he should redo the analysis to make sure.

9. Probably so. For a variety of reasons, states that are geographically close may be more likely to have similar legislative records.

10. No. The regression model makes no assumptions about the distribution of the independent variables.

11. With a sample of that size, there's little need to be concerned about the distribution of the dependent variable.

Chapter 7

1. This is a case of extreme multicollinearity. Age is merely the difference between year of survey and year of birth, a linear function.

2. It's unlikely that years of schooling would be highly correlated with the other variables in the model, so there's no problem getting good estimates for this variable.

3. Looking at two-way correlations is not enough. There could still be high correlations among larger sets of variables.

4. It's likely that there are high correlations among these variables. When all three are put in the regression at the same time, none of them might be statistically significant even though they would show up as significant one at a time. She should check tolerances and, if necessary, delete one or more of the variables from the equation.

5. Because the main goal is prediction, it doesn't matter much if there is multicollinearity. His results do suggest, however, that he might get nearly as good predictions with fewer variables in the model, which might be desirable.

6. The low tolerance suggests that multicollinearity is a problem here. These results could be quite unstable.

Chapter 8

1. The R^2 won't change at all. Subtracting the mean and dividing by the standard deviation is an example of a *linear* transformation, which has no effect on the model fit.

2. Transforming the dependent variable may help with hetero-scedasticity but will make the regression coefficients very hard to interpret. It would be better to use some other method for dealing with the heteroscedasticity.

3. $100(e^{.50} - 1) = 65\%$. Unemployed women spend 65% more time on housework than employed women, controlling for other variables in the model.

4. The model should also contain z.

5. No. You should delete the age-squared term and then see if age is significant.

6. The omitted category probably has too few people for comparisons to be reliable. An overall test for the set of dummies is desirable. It would also be better to make Republican or Democrat the omitted category.

7. The interaction of education and minority classification is highly significant, indicating that the effect of educational level on salary depends on whether one is a minority or not. The payoff for a year of schooling for nonminorities is $4,312. The payoff for a year of schooling for minorities is $(4,312 - 2,725) = \$1,587$.

References

Allison, Paul D. (1984). *Event history analysis*. Beverly Hills, CA: Sage.

Allison, Paul D. (1995). *Survival analysis using the SAS system: A practical guide*. Cary, NC: SAS Institute Inc.

Arbuckle, James L. (1998). *Amos users' guide*. Chicago: SmallWaters Corp.

Bollen, Kenneth A. (1989). *Structural equations with latent variables*. New York: Wiley.

Bryk, Anthony S., & Raudenbush, Stephen W. (1992). *Hierarchical linear models*. Newbury Park, CA: Sage.

Byrne, Barbara M. (1994). *Structural equation modeling with EQS and EQS/Windows*. Thousand Oaks, CA: Sage.

Chatterjee, Samprit & Price, Bertram. (1991). *Regression analysis by example*. New York: Wiley.

Cox, David R. (1972). Regression models and life tables. *Journal of the Royal Statistical Society, Series B, 34*, 187-202.

Davis, James A., & Smith, Tom W. (1997). *General Social Surveys, 1972-1996*. Ann Arbor, MI: Inter-University Consortium for Political and Social Research.

Draper, Norman R., & Smith, Harry. (1998). *Applied regression analysis* (3rd ed.). New York: Wiley.

Duncan, Otis Dudley. (1975). *Introduction to structural equation models*. New York: Academic Press.

Fox, John. (1997). *Applied regression analysis, linear models and related methods*. Thousand Oaks, CA: Sage.

Frankfort-Nachmias, Chava. (1997). *Social statistics for a diverse society*. Thousand Oaks, CA: Pine Forge Press.

Greene, William F. (1997). *Econometric analysis*. Upper Saddle River, NJ: Prentice Hall.

Gujarati, Damodar. (1995). *Basic econometrics*. New York: McGraw-Hill.

Haggard, Ernest A. (1958). *Intraclass correlation and the analysis of variance*. New York: Dryden.

Hayduk, Leslie A. (1988). *Structural equation modeling with LISREL: Essentials and advances*. Baltimore: Johns Hopkins University Press.

Iversen, Gudmund R., & Norpoth, Helmut. (1987). *Analysis of variance*. Newbury Park, CA: Sage.

Jöreskog, Karl G. (1997). *LISREL 8 user's reference guide*. Chicago: Scientific Software.

Kim, Jae-On, & Mueller, Charles W. (1978a). *Factor analysis*. Beverly Hills, CA: Sage.

Kim, Jae-On, & Mueller, Charles W. (1978b). *Introduction to factor analysis*. Beverly Hills, CA: Sage.

Kingston, Paul W., & Nock, Steven L. (1987). Time together among dual-earner couples. *American Sociological Review, 52*, 391-400.

Kleinbaum, David G., Kupper, Lawrence L., Muller, Keith E., & Nizam, Azhar. (1998). *Applied regression analysis and other multivariable methods* (3rd ed.). Pacific Grove, CA: Duxbury.

Kreft, Ida G. G., & De Leeuw, Jan. (1998). *Introducing multilevel modeling*. Thousand Oaks, CA: Sage.

Lewis-Beck, Michael S. (1995). *Data analysis*. Thousand Oaks, CA: Sage.

Link, Bruce G. (1987). Understanding labeling effects in the area of mental disorders: An assessment of the effects of expectations of rejection. *American Sociological Review, 52*, 96-112.

Long, J. Scott. (1997). *Regression models for categorical and limited dependent variables.* Thousand Oaks, CA: Sage.

McClendon, McKee J. (1994). *Multiple regression and causal analysis.* Itasca, IL: Peacock.

Menard, Scott. (1995). *Applied logistic regression analysis.* Thousand Oaks, CA: Sage.

Mendenhall, William M., & Sincich, Terry. (1996). *A second course in statistics: Regression analysis.* Upper Saddle River, NJ: Prentice Hall.

Phillips, Julie A. (1997). Variation in African-American homicide rates: An assessment of potential explanations. *Criminology, 34*, 527-559.

Ross, Catherine E., & Wu, Chia-ling. (1995). The links between education and health. *American Sociological Review, 60*, 719-745.

Seber, George A. F., & Wild, C. J. (1989). *Nonlinear regression.* New York: Wiley.

Tuch, Steven A. (1987). Urbanism, region, and tolerance revisited: The case of racial prejudice. *American Sociological Review, 52*, 504-510.

Wharton, Amy S., & Baron, James N. (1987). So happy together: The impact of gender segregation on men at work. *American Sociological Review, 52*, 574-587.

Wildt, Albert R., & Ahtola, Olli T. (1978). *Analysis of covariance.* Beverly Hills, CA: Sage.

Willerman, L., Schultz, R., Rutledge, J. N., & Bigler, E. (1991). In vivo brain size and intelligence. *Intelligence, 15*, 223-228.

Index